Financing Higher Education: Strategies After Tax Reform

Richard E. Anderson, *Editor*
Columbia University and National Center
for Postsecondary Governance and Finance

Joel W. Meyerson, *Editor*
Coopers & Lybrand and National Center
for Postsecondary Governance and Finance

NEW DIRECTIONS FOR HIGHER EDUCATION
MARTIN KRAMER, *Editor-in-Chief*
University of California, Berkeley

Number 58, Summer 1987

Paperback sourcebooks in
The Jossey-Bass Higher Education Series

Ministry of Education, Ontario
Information Centre, 13th Floor,
Mowat Block, Queen's Park,
Toronto, Ont.   M7A 1L2

Jossey-Bass Inc., Publishers
San Francisco • London

Richard E. Anderson, Joel W. Meyerson (eds.).
Financing Higher Education: Strategies After Tax Reform.
New Directions for Higher Education, no. 58.
Volume XV, number 2.
San Francisco: Jossey-Bass, 1987.

New Directions for Higher Education
Martin Kramer, *Editor-in-Chief*

Copyright © 1987 by Jossey-Bass Inc., Publishers
and
Jossey-Bass Limited

Copyright under International, Pan American, and Universal Copyright Conventions. All rights reserved. No part of this issue may be reproduced in any form—except for brief quotation (not to exceed 500 words) in a review or professional work—without permission in writing from the publishers.

New Directions for Higher Education is published quarterly by Jossey-Bass Inc., Publishers (publication number USPS 990-880). *New Directions* is numbered sequentially—please order extra copies by sequential number. The volume and issue numbers above are included for the convenience of libraries. Second-class postage paid at San Francisco, California, and at additional mailing offices. POSTMASTER: Send address changes to Jossey-Bass Inc., Publishers, 433 California Street, San Francisco, California 94104.

Editorial correspondence should be sent to the Editor-in-Chief, Martin Kramer, 2807 Shasta Road, Berkeley, California 94708.

Library of Congress Catalog Card Number LC 85-644752

International Standard Serial Number ISSN 0271-0560

International Standard Book Number ISBN 1-55542-963-7

Cover art by WILLI BAUM

Manufactured in the United States of America

Ordering Information

The paperback sourcebooks listed below are published quarterly and can be ordered either by subscription or single copy.

Subscriptions cost $48.00 per year for institutions, agencies, and libraries. Individuals can subscribe at the special rate of $36.00 per year *if payment is by personal check*. (Note that the full rate of $48.00 applies if payment is by institutional check, even if the subscription is designated for an individual.) Standing orders are accepted.

Single copies are available at $11.95 when payment accompanies order. (California, New Jersey, New York, and Washington, D.C., residents please include appropriate sales tax.) For billed orders, cost per copy is $11.95 plus postage and handling.

Substantial discounts are offered to organizations and individuals wishing to purchase bulk quantities of Jossey-Bass sourcebooks. Please inquire.

Please note that these prices are for the academic year 1986-1987 and are subject to change without notice. Also, some titles may be out of print and therefore not available for sale.

To ensure correct and prompt delivery, all orders must give either the *name of an individual* or an *official purchase order number*. Please submit your order as follows:

Subscriptions: specify series and year subscription is to begin.
Single Copies: specify sourcebook code (such as, HE1) and first two words of title.

Mail orders for United States and Possessions, Australia, New Zealand, Canada, Latin America, and Japan to:
Jossey-Bass Inc., Publishers
433 California Street
San Francisco, California 94104

Mail orders for all other parts of the world to:
Jossey-Bass Limited
28 Banner Street
London EC1Y 8QE

New Directions for Higher Education Series
Martin Kramer, *Editor-in-Chief*

HE1 *Facilitating Faculty Development,* Mervin Freedman
HE2 *Strategies for Budgeting,* George Kaludis
HE3 *Services for Students,* Joseph Katz

HE4	*Evaluating Learning and Teaching,* C. Robert Pace
HE5	*Encountering the Unionized University,* Jack H. Schuster
HE6	*Implementing Field Experience Education,* John Duley
HE7	*Avoiding Conflict in Faculty Personnel Practices,* Richard Peairs
HE8	*Improving Statewide Planning,* James L. Wattenbarger, Louis W. Bender
HE9	*Planning the Future of the Undergraduate College,* Donald G. Trites
HE10	*Individualizing Education by Learning Contracts,* Neal R. Berte
HE11	*Meeting Women's New Educational Needs,* Clare Rose
HE12	*Strategies for Significant Survival,* Clifford T. Stewart, Thomas R. Harvey
HE13	*Promoting Consumer Protection for Students,* Joan S. Stark
HE14	*Expanding Recurrent and Nonformal Education,* David Harman
HE15	*A Comprehensive Approach to Institutional Development,* William Bergquist, William Shoemaker
HE16	*Improving Educational Outcomes,* Oscar Lenning
HE17	*Renewing and Evaluating Teaching,* John A. Centra
HE18	*Redefining Service, Research, and Teaching,* Warren Bryan Martin
HE19	*Managing Turbulence and Change,* John D. Millett
HE20	*Increasing Basic Skills by Developmental Studies,* John E. Roueche
HE21	*Marketing Higher Education,* David W. Barton, Jr.
HE22	*Developing and Evaluating Administrative Leadership,* Charles F. Fisher
HE23	*Admitting and Assisting Students After Bakke,* Alexander W. Astin, Bruce Fuller, Kenneth C. Green
HE24	*Institutional Renewal Through the Improvement of Teaching,* Jerry G. Gaff
HE25	*Assuring Access for the Handicapped,* Martha Ross Redden
HE26	*Assessing Financial Health,* Carol Frances, Sharon L. Coldren
HE27	*Building Bridges to the Public,* Louis T. Benezet, Frances W. Magnusson
HE28	*Preparing for the New Decade,* Larry W. Jones, Franz A. Nowotny
HE29	*Educating Learners of All Ages,* Elinor Greenberg, Kathleen M. O'Donnell, William Bergquist
HE30	*Managing Facilities More Effectively,* Harvey H. Kaiser
HE31	*Rethinking College Responsibilities for Values,* Mary Louise McBee
HE32	*Resolving Conflict in Higher Education,* Jane E. McCarthy
HE33	*Professional Ethics in University Administration,* Ronald H. Stein, M. Carlota Baca
HE34	*New Approaches to Energy Conservation,* Sidney G. Tickton
HE35	*Management Science Applications to Academic Administration,* James A. Wilson
HE36	*Academic Leaders as Managers,* Robert H. Atwell, Madeleine F. Green
HE37	*Designing Academic Program Reviews,* Richard F. Wilson
HE38	*Successful Responses to Financial Difficulties,* Carol Frances
HE39	*Priorities for Academic Libraries,* Thomas J. Galvin, Beverly P. Lynch
HE40	*Meeting Student Aid Needs in a Period of Retrenchment,* Martin Kramer
HE41	*Issues in Faculty Personnel Policies,* Jon W. Fuller
HE42	*Management Techniques for Small and Specialized Institutions,* Andrew J. Falender, John C. Merson
HE43	*Meeting the New Demand for Standards,* Jonathan R. Warren
HE44	*The Expanding Role of Telecommunications in Higher Education,* Pamela J. Tate, Marilyn Kressel
HE45	*Women in Higher Education Administration,* Adrian Tinsley, Cynthia Secor, Sheila Kaplan

HE46 *Keeping Graduate Programs Responsive to National Needs,*
        Michael J. Pelczar, Jr., Lewis C. Solomon
HE47 *Leadership Roles of Chief Academic Officers,* David G. Brown
HE48 *Financial Incentives for Academic Quality,* John Folger
HE49 *Leadership and Institutional Renewal,* Ralph M. Davis
HE50 *Applying Corporate Management Strategies,* Roger J. Flecher
HE51 *Incentive for Faculty Vitality,* Roger G. Baldwin
HE52 *Making the Budget Process Work,* David J. Berg, Gerald M. Skogley
HE53 *Managing College Enrollments,* Don Hossler
HE54 *Institutional Revival: Case Histories,* Douglas W. Steeples
HE55 *Crisis Management in Higher Education,* Hal Hoverland, Pat McInturff,
        C. E. Tapie Rohm, Jr.
HE56 *Managing Programs for Learning Outside the Classroom,*
        Patricia Senn Breivik
HE57 *Creating Career Programs in a Liberal Arts Context,* Mary Ann F. Rehnke

Contents

Editors' Notes 1
Richard E. Anderson, Joel W. Meyerson

1. **Tax Reform and Higher Education** 9
Gail Franck, Richard E. Anderson, Clark Bernard
Tax reform will affect colleges and universities in many ways, including fund-raising methods, operating costs, and means of tuition payment.

2. **Capital Needs in Higher Education** 21
Harvey H. Kaiser
The rapid deterioration of plant and equipment in higher education institutions necessitates quick action by colleges to assess capital needs.

3. **Tax Reform and the Bond Market** 33
David C. Clapp
The tax-exempt bond market continues to be unsettled, but many issues have been resolved by the Tax Reform Act of 1986.

4. **Tax-Exempt Leasing for Colleges and Universities** 41
C. Gregory H. Eden
Tax-exempt leasing is emerging as an attractive and practical option for financing equipment and facilities.

5. **Financing Tuition: Are Prepayment Plans the Right Answer?** 53
Loren Hart
Because higher education is becoming more expensive every year, there is a great need for new methods of financing.

6. **Equity Financing: Research Partnerships** 67
Michael B. Goldstein
Managing and exploiting intellectual property is a great challenge for the contemporary university administrator.

7. **Equity Financing: Real Estate** 77
Richard Thomas, Jonathan Davies
Many small, private colleges are examining aggressive ways of economically developing their land and other physical assets.

8. **Making It All Work: Sound Financial Management** 87
William F. Massy
Tax reform increases the need for integrated financial planning of nontraditional income-generating activities and of capital sources and uses.

Index 103

Editors' Notes

The landscape of higher education capital finance is rapidly changing. Once limited to financing the physical plant, today it includes all assets and aspects of institutional life—physical, financial, and intellectual. Once its focus was primarily on debt and equity. Today it encompasses a wide range of approaches and techniques including pooled debt, capital leases, futures contracts, equity investments, and research partnerships. And at one time in the not-too-distant past, it was within the purview of investment bankers, accountants, and financial officers. Now it is the prerogative of the entire academic community. In short, the scope of capital finance has expanded dramatically in recent years to include the "larger" academy and all its participants.

A New Perspective

Why has this happened? Why have the definition and requirements of American higher education finance broadened? There are several reasons. First, the general business environment has changed rapidly and has been characterized in the last five years by a sharp downturn in economic activity followed by a long period of economic expansion. Second, our national higher education policy has been wildly erratic, highlighted initially by incentives and followed quickly by disincentives for privatization of American higher education. As a result, there is now no clear federal policy for funding America's basic research establishment. Third, costs are rising rapidly, especially in operations attributable to the following: (1) the need to repair and renew buildings built during the fifteen-year construction boom after World War II; (2) rapid technology turnover and the need to replace obsolete scientific and research equipment; and (3) the growing sophistication and cost of management technology, notably computer systems, distributed data processing, and voice/data communications systems. Fourth, there is a developing need to replace or augment shrinking revenue sources, such as tuition and fees and government contracts, with new sources of funds.

The material presented herein was gathered pursuant to a grant from the Office of Educational Research and Improvement/Department of Education (OERI/ED). However, the opinions expressed herein do not necessarily reflect the position or policy of the OERI/ED and no official endorsement by the OERI/ED should be inferred.

These changes have led to a reevaluation of institutional capital. Exactly what are a college's assets and their value? How should they be financed? Are institutional assets adequate or inadequate to fulfill a college's mission?

Superimposed on these issues is the problem of tax reform. In 1986 Congress passed and the president signed the most sweeping changes in the country's tax code in thirty-two years. This legislation sent shock waves through the capital markets and through the tax-paying and gift-giving public.

In order to explore these new opportunities and challenges in financing American higher education in the post-tax reform era, the Forum for College Financing Alternatives (a research project of the National Center for Postsecondary Governance and Finance) invited fifty leaders in higher education finance and management to a conference in Annapolis in October 1986. The papers presented at that conference form the core of this book.

An important theme that emerged from the conference is that any approach to analyzing academic capital must encompass all the assets of an institution—physical, financial, and human. Physical capital is the land, buildings, and equipment. Financial capital is the endowment, investments, reserves, and other financial property. Human capital is people: faculty and staff, researchers, and students. Together these constitute the capital resources, the wealth of an institution. How effectively they are managed and financed determines, in large measure, how successful an institution is.

Tax Reform

The Tax Reform Act of 1986 has completely overhauled the American tax system. Its changes are so sweeping that its impact on the economy and American society in general can only be guessed. One thing is certain, however: The Act absolutely changes the rules of the game in higher education finance. In the first chapter, Franck, Anderson, and Bernard discuss some of the provisions in the new law that have the most significant potential impact on colleges and universities.

The new tax legislation affects the financing of each class of academic assets. First, consider the physical assets. New restrictions on tax-exempt financing will make it more expensive for certain institutions to finance facilities and equipment. Moreover, these limits apply primarily to private higher education, which raises money in financial markets and may, in the words of Senator Daniel Patrick Moynihan (D, NY) "emphatically tilt" a heretofore level playing field in favor of the public sector.

Then there are the financial resources. The cost of giving is going up. This is attributable to lower tax rates on personal income, which will increase the after-tax of giving, as well as to less favorable treatment of gifts of appreciated property. These two factors will make building the endowment more difficult in the future.

Finally, the university's greatest assets—the human assets—must be examined. Tax reform has had a particularly unpleasant effect on students and their families. The cost of education will be increasing. The new restrictions on income shifting and other forms of tax-advantaged savings make saving for college more costly as well. Limiting deductibility of interest on student loans makes borrowing for tuition more expensive. And treating certain scholarships and fellowships as taxable income likewise increases the cost of attending the university.

The students are not the only human assets of the university to feel the effects of tax reform. As the cost of attending college increases, the benefits of working there diminish. Limits on 403(b) retirement plans have been imposed. Nondiscrimination rules for benefit programs have been toughened. And even the cost of faculty housing may rise.

Scope of the Problem

Before exploring new approaches to capital finance, it may be helpful to gauge the extent of the problem. Kaiser does this in Chapter Two. Focusing on physical capital, he poses the question: Is there a "crisis of capital" in higher education? How undercapitalized are America's colleges and universities? It is difficult to answer these questions because of the dearth of quantitative data on the subject. Some data is, however, available. Twenty percent of all campus facilities are estimated to be in unsatisfactory condition. This translates to $40 to $50 billion of deferred maintenance nationally. Four to five billion dollars is needed annually for capital renewal; an additional $3 billion may also be needed each year. Colleges spend on average 10 to 11 percent of operating budgets on maintenance, the same level they spent a decade ago despite many factors justifying a substantially higher level of funding.

The picture is equally, if not more, sobering for scientific equipment. According to one National Science Foundation study, the age of university research equipment is twice that of commercial laboratories. Another NSF study shows that 24 percent of academic research equipment in the computer and physical sciences and engineering is obsolete, and only 15 percent is state of the art.

Far more information is needed before a clear picture emerges of capital requirements for existing and new facilities and equipment as well as resources available to meet these requirements. Present data, however, suggest that the needs are great and that available funds will be increasingly inadequate.

Five of the chapters in this sourcebook explore some of the most promising areas for effective capital financing. The covered subjects include debt and near-debt financing, equity financing, and tuition financing.

Debt and Near-Debt Financing

In Chapter Three, Clapp explores traditional and novel debt instruments. Next, Eden explores a not-quite-debt but attractive way to finance equipment and facilities in Chapter Four.

Debt. In the last ten years, colleges took advantage of a remarkable array of new debt instruments. As a result, colleges have had considerable flexibility and have made significant progress in meeting their capital requirements. The Tax Reform Act of 1986 rolls back the financing options open to colleges. New restrictions on private activity bonds may limit opportunities for tax-exempt financing and make debt more expensive. New caps on tax-exempt financing by private institutions may increase their costs and diminish their competitiveness with public institutions. New limits on the use of bond proceeds may impair certain activities, particularly research, and limits on amounts paid for issuance may make financing less available for small projects and small institutions. New arbitrage requirements practically eliminate arbitrage profiteering from the reinvestment of bond proceeds. And new restrictions limit advance refundings. Tax reform limits the ability of public and private colleges to satisfy their capital needs. Private institutions are more severely hampered and may be even more so in the future as a result of the designation of their bonds as private activity bonds, which thereby exposes these institutions to other possible restrictions on this form of debt.

Near-Debt. Tax-exempt leasing provides *public* colleges with an attractive way to finance equipment and facilities. Moreover, many of its benefits may still be in place after the dust of tax reform settles. A tax-exempt lease, sometimes called a municipal lease, is a tax-exempt conditional sales contract in which title to property passes directly to the college. Interest earned by investors is generally tax-exempt. Moreover, it allows the institution to record the transaction as an operating expense rather than a debt obligation. To minimize the possibility of nonpayment (nonappropriation), colleges usually must demonstrate that the leased property is essential.

Benefits to colleges of tax-exempt leases include ownership of the property, off-balance-sheet financing, and generally lower financing costs. Benefits to investors include tax-exempt interest income, shorter terms, and higher real returns.

Although the Tax Reform of 1986 sought to curtail the use of tax-exempt financing, tax-exempt leases escaped relatively unscathed. This is because they are treated as public purpose obligations under the Act and subject to relatively few restrictions. However, costs to colleges may increase because interest payments to investors are likely to rise and arbitrage earnings will disappear.

Tuition Financing

Changes in the tax law that make saving and paying for college more expensive—as well as the recent runup in tuition and cutback in loan programs—have led many institutions to consider ways to make tuition more affordable. In Chapter Five, Hart discusses an interesting alternative. Prepayment plans allow parents to guarantee a future level of tuition by prepaying the present value (usually a fraction of the future value) of tuition now. It is, essentially, a form of tax-advantaged savings for parents, since they hope not to be taxed on the gain of their prepayment. Benefits to colleges include early receipt of funds and "locking in" future students; risks include underestimating future tuition (on which payment amounts are based) and poor investment return on prepayments. Prepayment plans also raise many tax questions that, up to now, have not been resolved. Chief among these is the treatment of appreciation (Is it imputed interest?) if the designated student does not enroll and prepaid amounts are withdrawn or transferred to another student.

Prepayment plans have been proposed by single institutions, consortia of similar institutions, states, and on a national basis. Institutions have had the greatest success in getting their plans up and running, and several states are on the verge of implementing their plans. National plans are being drawn up by several large investment firms and other private organizations. This activity raises several public policy issues, most notably: Will state plans (which have the greatest momentum now and are not generally portable from state to state) lead to the balkanization of American higher education? Will focus on this form of financing detract attention from the price and cost of education and student aid? A spirited public discussion on these topics in progress.

Equity Financing

Equity financing allows colleges to own and participate in the earnings of a range of enterprises. Goldstein in Chapter Six shows how to fully capitalize on an institution's most valuable asset—its intellectual capital. In Chapter Seven, Thomas and Davies discuss how equity investments, usually in real estate or other real property not directly related to an institution's mission, represent an aggressive but popular approach to higher education funding.

Equity Investments. Increasing capital requirements and constrained resources have prompted many institutions to seek new ways to maximize their long-term wealth. Recently, institutions have started to diversify their portfolios to include such nontraditional investments as venture capital funds and oil and gas partnerships. Institutions are now starting to consider direct equity investments, notably real estate development.

Past participation in real estate has generally been limited to the sale of contributions of real estate for cash (for reinvestment in stocks and bonds) or investment in mortgage-backed securities. Colleges have forgone real estate income and appreciation in favor of less risky steady-stream investments.

Colleges that are interested in real estate investments seek to acquire property through contributions and participation agreements. Bargain sales are a particularly attractive form of real estate contribution. In exchange for a gift of property, a donor receives a cash consideration from the college (considerably less than the value of the property) plus a tax deduction for the contribution. In many instances, the donor receives a greater after-tax cash flow from the bargain sale than from a traditional market-value sale. However, the returns may be less in the future because of tax reform.

Participation agreements allow colleges to partake of the benefits of real estate ownership. Popular types of agreements include participation leases (in which the college leases property to a third party), participation financing (where a college loans funds to real estate investors), and joint venture participation (in which the college invests in a partnership).

Real estate investment raises several tax issues for colleges. In an extreme case, real estate activities can grow so much that they dominate the institution and overshadow its educational mission, causing the college to lose its tax-exempt status. Even in an average case, the college will probably have to pay unrelated business income tax, particularly if the property is debt financed. And it is important to note that Congress and the business community are increasingly concerned about colleges and nonprofit organizations engaging in for-profit activities. Restrictive legislation may be forthcoming.

Research Partnerships. Intellectual property, the knowledge created by academic pursuits, may be a college's most valuable capital asset. Up to now, efforts to exploit this knowledge have been limited by the institution's reluctance to engage in business activities and the belief that commerce is inconsistent with instruction and research. Even when colleges tried to realize economic gain for their research through licensure and royalty arrangements, they received only a fraction of the true value of their scientific discoveries.

Research partnerships provide an opportunity for institutions to capture the value of their intellectual property. Under such an arrangement, a college agrees with a business organization to create a new entity. The college brings scientific knowledge to the enterprise, and the business firm brings financial and marketing know-how. Together, they share in any economic gain that accrues. If the partnership is successful, the college may claim its share of earnings or sell its interest in the partnership.

Benefits of research partnerships to colleges include better access to the latest scientific equipment—the partnership can raise money, acquire equipment, lease the equipment to the institution, and at the end of the lease term, donate it to the institution. And under the new tax code, this may be increasingly advantageous to both the institution and the partnership. Research partnerships are particularly beneficial to public institutions, for whom acquisitions of scientific equipment is usually a cumbersome process. Also, by allowing faculty to share in the equity of the partnership, institutions can reduce the brain drain to the commercial world.

But research partnerships are a mixed blessing. The institution may be liable for partnership debts, negligence, and unforeseen events. The institution might insulate itself from some of these problems by creating an intermediary agency to serve as a buffer between the institution and the partnership. These partnerships, if profitable, will almost always be subject to unrelated business income tax. There is a potential conflict of interest and identity for faculty participating in the partnership—can a professor serve two masters? Any business enterprise requires some degree of confidentiality for its proprietary information, but is this consistent with the academic ethos of free exchange of ideas? Finally, the university may be well managed as a university, but its managers may not be competent to oversee a potentially complex commercial enterprise.

Making It All Work

In the concluding chapter, Massy shows that effective financial management requires a new approach to financial planning at colleges and universities. Institutions must fully integrate planning for sources and uses of capital and, at the same time, evaluate the impact of capital funding alternatives on operations. Key sources of capital include operating surpluses, prepayments, private gifts and grants, government gifts and grants, government appropriations, research arrangements, debt, and leasing. Uses of capital include renewal and construction of facilities, equipment, student and faculty housing, student loans, working capital, and investment of funds.

Integrated financial planning is ambitious: It involves consolidating major planning activities into a single plan. Elements include planning for operations (projecting income and expenses of current operations and investments); planning for academic facilities (setting project priorities and analyzing these priorities in the context of funds available for academic facilities) and planning for debt (building a debt structure that reflects all available debt instruments, tax-exempt and taxable, and pooling of institutional debt to achieve an optimal mix of rates, maturities, and cash flow). Financing operations and capital will be adversely affected by the impact of the Tax Reform Act of 1986 on the funding and costs of higher education.

Integrating planning for capital and planning for operations will precipitate a new look at the relationship between financial and program goals and decisions. It will also promote analysis of the real—and perhaps unanticipated—costs of new financing strategies. It will, if successful, lead to a realistic assessment of the risks of leverage.

Acknowledgments

The symposium and this sourcebook would not have been possible without the assistance of many people and organizations. The presenters did a superb job of highlighting the major issues and focusing the discussion. The reactors to the presentations, and the entire group of participants, raised a variety of new considerations and brought a diverse set of perceptions to the problems and opportunities that lie ahead. Gail Franck and Douglas Wofford were particularly helpful in arranging the symposium as was the staff of the Historic Inns. Of course, none of this would have been possible without the support of the Office of Educational Research and Improvement of the U.S. Department of Education. Salvatore Corrallo has been a good critic of our work, a critic in the best sense of the word. Finally, Jonathan C. Derek has been an invaluable colleague in helping us put together the manuscript. He not only helped reshape our words but he challenged our concepts and thinking.

Richard E. Anderson
Joel W. Meyerson
Editors

Richard E. Anderson is chairman of the Department of Higher and Adult Education at Teachers College, Columbia University, and codirector of the Forum for College Financing Alternatives, a project of the National Center for Postsecondary Governance and Finance.

Joel W. Meyerson is director of the National Higher Education Practice of Coopers & Lybrand and codirector of the Forum for College Financing Alternatives, a project of the National Center for Postsecondary Goverance and Finance.

Tax reform will affect colleges and universities in many ways, including fund-raising methods, operating costs, and means of tuition payment.

Tax Reform and Higher Education

Gail Franck, Richard E. Anderson, Clark Bernard

The heart of tax reform is the reduction of tax rates and the broadening of the tax base through the elimination of many deductions, tax credits, and other forms of tax reduction. Through these and other changes, the Internal Revenue Code of 1986 will affect every individual and business substantially. The effects on colleges and universities are both direct, such as the extension of nondiscrimination rules to institutional retirement plans, and indirect, as in the elimination of the tax benefits of nongrantor trusts.

This chapter will provide a general overview of these effects on higher education. The new law can be viewed in terms of its effect on institutional revenues and expenditures.

Higher Education Revenues and the New Tax Law

Institutional revenues derive primarily from five sources: tuition and fees, charitable contributions, debt financing, governmental appropriations, and endowment income.

Tuition and Fees. Tuition is paid from parental and student income, savings, student loans, and financial aid. The new tax law has a direct impact in each of these areas.

Family Income. The multiple bracket system with a top rate of 50 percent has been replaced by two brackets of 15 and 28 percent and an additional surtax for high income taxpayers that eliminates the advantage of the initial 15 percent bracket. The phase-in of the surtax creates, in effect, a 33 percent marginal rate. Married individuals filing jointly, for example, will be in the 33 percent bracket if they have incomes approximately between $72,000 and $150,000.

The lower tax rates should create more disposable income, some of which may be earmarked for higher educational expenses. On the other hand, the elimination of many deductions and the curtailment of others will eliminate many of these gains. Families in higher income brackets will lose the benefits of some traditional tax shelters. Higher-income taxpayers may also be subject to an alternative minimum tax (AMT). Many items deductible from regular income must be added back as tax preference items in the calculation of the AMT. The AMT is calculated at a flat rate of 21 percent. A taxpayer must pay the AMT if the AMT liability exceeds the regular tax liability.

Independent students, most of whom will be in the lower tax bracket and are almost always without tax shelters, should keep more income after taxes under the 1986 law. For dependent students, however, it is a different story. Under the old law both students and parents could take the personal exemption deduction of the student on their respective returns, provided certain support conditions were met. Now, although the value of the personal exemption is increasing, it may only be taken on one return. Consequently, if a dependent student earns over $4,000 and may be claimed on his parents' return, it is likely that he will pay more taxes under the new law.

The effects of these changes on after-tax income are mixed. However, to the extent that the Act achieves its avowed goals of revenue neutrality and of shifting the tax burden from individuals to corporations, the average family should have more after-tax income with which to pay college bills.

Savings. Traditionally, many upper-middle income families have saved for higher education by shifting savings into the names of their children under the Uniform Gifts to Minors Act or by putting funds in educational (short-term grantor) trusts. The new tax code expands the taxpayer's income base by making the family a single taxpaying unit. Until the age of fourteen, a child's unearned income is taxed in part at the parents' rate. Although the new rules on personal deductions vary for earned and unearned income, the general result is that children's unearned income in excess of $1,000 is taxable at the parents' marginal rate. Furthermore, the income generated by short-term grantor trusts will be taxed at the grantor's rate.

Parents may still use a 2503(c) trust to transfer income to a minor child and pay taxes at the child's rate rather than their own. Under this section, however, the funds must revert to the child at age twenty-one. At this time the child has full control of the funds and may (or may not) use them for educational purposes.

Parents who want to save for education without using trusts might consider giving funds to their children and invest the funds in securities with low payout but high potential appreciation that can be sold after the minor turns fourteen. The children would then be taxed but at the lower rate, presumably 15 percent. Although the appreciation of zero coupon bonds is taxed as if it produced an annual yield, Series EE Savings Bonds, which sell at a deep discount, are not taxed in this way. As such, Savings Bonds can be used to delay unearned income until the child is fourteen. However, parents are limited to an annual investment of $15,000 ($30,000 face value) in these bonds per child. Another strategy is to buy single premium life insurance from which the parent can "borrow out" the earnings (and in some policies, a large portion of the principal) at a low interest rate. No taxes are due unless the policy is surrendered. Even though this sounds attractive, it is not a very flexible form of savings, and there are risks. There are often high surrender fees in the early years. Moreover, the growth in the policy value is dependent on the success of the companies' money managers. When cautioning families on this technique, one financial adviser quoted in the *Wall Street Journal* observed that tax reform didn't turn such people into good money managers overnight.

Loans. As noted earlier, many deductions have been lost in tax reform. The most important of these for many taxpayers is that consumer interest expenses will no longer be deductible after the phase-out period ending in 1989. Interest on mortgages for both first and second homes and certain interest on debt that is linked to investment income may (with some exceptions) be used to reduce taxable income; and there are restrictions. The interest is only deductible on loans made up to the actual cost of the initial purchase plus improvements; interest on loans made against appreciation of the property is not generally deductible. Rollover gains from previous homes are not included as part of the cost basis. A beneficial exception for higher education is that individuals may borrow on the full value of their home and retain the deduction for the interest expense if the proceeds of these loans are used for educational or medical purposes.

The obvious implication of these changes is that unless higher education debt is mortgage based, the cost to students and parents will rise dramatically. This issue is being challenged in two ways. Some higher education officials are trying to reintroduce all educational debt in the deductible category as the new law undergoes technical corrections. Others are exploring ways by which state and institutional loan programs can become mortgaged-backed debt. Some plans have already been announced.

Financial Aid. Under the new law, the exclusion for scholarships and fellowships is limited to amounts received and actually used by degree candidates for tuition, books, and fees. Amounts received by degree candidates for room, board, and incidental expenses will be taxable to the student, as is the full amount of any grant received by a nondegree student.

The taxable portion of any scholarship will be treated as earned income. As earned income, it may be offset by the standard deduction, which will be $3,000 for a single filer in the 1988 tax year. If the student is not claimed as a dependent on the parents' return, the personal exemption of $1,950 in 1988 would also be available to offset any taxable scholarship amounts. Thus, only large scholarships would create tax liability for most students.

A hidden consequence of the loss of the double claim on personal exemptions is that there will be considerably less incentive for students to remain dependent. Most tests of financial independence look to see if the prospective financial aid recipient was claimed as a dependent on the parents' return. In the new tax law, the tax savings to parents from the dependency claim is about half as great as under the old code. This reduction occurs in spite of the fact that the personal exemption will double over the next few years. Thus, we may see a surge of students claiming independent status.

The new law fails to define the reporting requirements associated with the granting of scholarship or fellowship funds. Although the IRS has no statutory authority to compel grantors to report scholarships to the government, such information would appear necessary to enforce the provision. Thus, future reporting requirements may ultimately increase the administrative costs associated with scholarship programs in universities and indirectly reduce total funds available for assistance.

The new tax law leaves unchanged the present tuition remission benefit. Employees of institutions of higher education are generally exempt from taxes on tuition remission if the statutory nondiscrimination rules are met. Note, however, that the benefit again applies only to tuition and required fees. Also, wage payments received by university employees who are students enrolled and regularly attending classes at the employer university are not subject to FICA tax under Internal Revenue Code Section 3121(b)(10).

The exclusion for nonuniversity employer-provided educational assistance is increased to $5,250 and has been extended retroactively for two years, from January 1, 1986, to December 31, 1987.

These new rules for scholarships and fellowships do not affect awards made before August 17, 1986. Scholarships awarded between August 17 and December 31, 1986, are subject to the old law, provided the money was used for 1986 expenses. New awards for 1987 are under the new rules.

Summary. The Tax Reform Act of 1986 will affect the tuition area of college and university revenues in many ways. The elimination of many brackets and the reductions of tax rates with the concurrent elimination of many deductions and means of income shifting will probably increase the cost of education for many families.

Charitable Contributions. Tax reform will have a substantial impact on the tax incentive to give at both the individual and corporate level. The changes in the treatment of charitable giving mandates a reevaluation by colleges and universities of their fund-raising strategies.

Reduction in Marginal Tax Rates. With the reduction in the top tax rate from 50 percent in 1986 to 38.5 percent in 1987 and 28 percent in 1988—along with a similar reduction from 46 to 34 percent for corporations—charitable contributions are more valuable to donors from a tax perspective in earlier rather than later years. The tax value of contributions will be greater in 1987 than in 1988, but lower marginal tax rates will still make contributing more expensive than it has been in the past. The long-range effect on the contribution base for tax-exempt organizations is not known with any certainty, but economists have generally predicted that an increase in the cost of contributing will reduce the level of contributions to some degree.

The new law also eliminates the deductibility of charitable contributions for nonitemizers. This may prove to be a disincentive for smaller donors, such as recent alumni.

Contributions of Property. Donors of property are entitled to deduct the full value of the property contributed. Under the new Act, the amount of untaxed appreciation (the difference between the original cost of the property and its market value) will be a tax preference item and could, in some circumstances, subject the donor to the alternative minimum tax (AMT) or increase the AMT if one is already due. Whether an individual (or corporation) will be subject to the AMT in any one year depends on the individual's overall tax profile.

Because most major donors are tax conscious and want to avoid an alternative minimum tax, it is likely that they would limit the amount of appreciated property contributed in any one year. In future years, however, donations of appreciated property might help donors avoid payment of new and higher taxes on capital gains that would otherwise be owed on the sale of the appreciated property.

The new law severely limits the ability to deduct losses on real estate investments under the so-called passive loss provision. As a result, some may want to contribute their real estate limited partnerships to tax-exempt institutions in order to get a tax deduction for the gift and also because there may be a limited ability to sell such interests. However, contributions of limited partnership interests raise at least two issues that must be resolved. First, the recipient institution should carefully evaluate the gift. Such gifts may carry hidden costs, such as calls for additional cash. Second, many partnerships are leveraged with debt. If nonprofit organizations, including colleges and universities, use debt to finance investments, the resulting income may be considered taxable as unrelated business income.

Estates and Gifts. Estate and gift taxes are relatively unchanged by the new code. In particular, the deductibility of charitable gifts is unlimited. With the concurrent changes in other areas, estates become a more valuable area for potential contributions. These changes create an opportunity that deserves renewed attention by colleges and universities.

Contributions of Equipment. Corporate donors continue to receive favorable treatment for contributions of research equipment. Their charitable deduction is equal to cost plus half the difference between cost and market value, up to twice the cost.

Other provisions of the new law provide additional incentives for corporations to donate equipment. For example, higher capital gains rates raise the tax cost of selling equipment used in the trade or business, making charitable contributions of such equipment relatively more attractive. And new rules requiring the capitalization of additional items into inventory costs will increase those costs and likewise increase the value of contributions of inventory items. Finally, a special rule provides an augmented charitable deduction for corporations that donate newly manufactured scientific equipment to a college or university for research in the physical or biological sciences.

Research and Experimentation Credit. The special corporate research and experimentation credit (R & E credit) for qualifying expenditures at universities and certain other organizations has been extended retroactively through 1988. It has, however, been reduced from 25 to 20 percent. Further, a separate 20 percent credit is allowed for funding basic research at universities and other scientific institutions, effective after December 31, 1986.

The continuation of the R & E credit, as one of the few special tax benefits left for corporations, should assist universities in garnering funding for qualifying projects.

Summary. Colleges and universities will probably find it more difficult to solicit contributions under the new law. The lower tax rates, the inclusion of the appreciated value of unrealized gains in calculating the AMT, and the nondeductibility of gifts for nonitemizers are the most serious changes. However, the new tax law looks favorably on corporate donations of equipment and research contracts. If an institution has a current working relationship with one or more corporations, institutional officials should consider how the tax law will affect the tax situation of those businesses.

Debt Financing. This section highlights some of the issues in higher education debt financing after tax reform. A much more thorough treatment is provided in Clapp's chapter (this volume).

The debt issues by state and local subdivisions are labeled governmental use bonds or private activity bonds, depending on the purpose for which the funds are raised. Funds raised to build a courthouse or buy police cars are obviously governmental use. Funds used to provide low-interest debt to private redevelopers of a city slum are private activity. Student loan bonds were previously, and continue to be, classified as private activity bonds. Unfortunately for private higher education, the debt of educational, scientific, charitable, and religious organizations—that is, 501(c)(3) organizations—will now be considered private activity debt.

To distinguish between governmental use and private activity bonds, the IRS uses several tests that relate to who will use or benefit from the proceeds of the debt and who is securing the debt. The percentage of the debt allowed to be used by or secured by private interest has been reduced. Under the old law, governmental use bonds could use 25 percent private collateral. That has now been lowered to 10 percent. The tests are even more restrictive for 501(c)(3) organizations that, to keep tax-exempt status, must meet a 5 percent standard. Student loan bonds receive special treatment and will be held to the 10 percent level. These more restrictive tests create obvious, although complicated, problems. For example, if tax-exempt debt is used to build a research facility that will house cooperative research with industry, the tax-exempt status of the entire debt issue may be jeopardized. Or, the construction of dormitories that include private franchises (such as leased cafeterias) may be ineligible for tax-exempt financing. It is even more essential under the new tax law that investment brokers and bond counsel be involved in the planning process early.

The new law places stricter limits on the amount of outstanding private activity debt a state may allow. This unified cap will be the greater of $75 per capita or $250 million until December 31, 1987. Thereafter, it will be the greater of $50 per capita or $150 million. This cap includes qualified student loan bonds. Fortunately for private colleges and universities, qualified 501(c)(3) bonds are specifically exempt from the unified volume cap.

Except for hospitals, all 501(c)(3) institutions are individually limited to $150 million of outstanding tax-exempt bonds. As a result, approximately twenty-five of the largest private universities will be effectively shut out of the tax-exempt bond market. Taxable debt is an alternative and has the advantage of being considerably more flexible, but the institutions will pay an additional two or more percentage points on such debt. Moreover, unless the law is changed, more private colleges will find themselves bumping up against the $150 million ceiling.

In an effort to control costs, both governmental use and private activity bonds are subject to a 2 percent cap on the cost of issuance. Although the stated purpose of this regulation is cost control, it is hard to imagine that it will be effective. Investment bankers will undoubtedly unbundle their services and charge separately for activities that were previously included in the cost of issuance.

Now that independent colleges and universities are included in the private use category, it could be more complicated to structure debt that serves both private and public sectors. As a result, some new cooperative ventures between the sectors may never get launched.

Finally, in an effort to control the abuse of tax-exempt debt to produce extra income, new arbitrage restrictions have been enacted. Issuers of debt generally do not need the full proceeds of the debt immediately. In addition, the lenders will often require that a reserve fund be established to help ensure payment of the debt. The unused portion of the debt and the reserve fund can, therefore, be invested. If tax-exempt issues invest in taxable bonds, the interest earned will almost always exceed the interest paid. This difference is called arbitrage income. The new tax law requires that almost all of this arbitrage income be rebated to the federal government. The loss of the arbitrage will raise the costs of every activity financed with tax-exempt debt.

Governmental Appropriations. Tax reform does not specifically impact governmental appropriations for colleges and universities. The tightening of the federal budget relating to social service expenditures (particularly higher education) and the predisposition of the federal government to move away from grants and federally subsidized programs all indicate that a cooler climate for federal appropriations will be with us for some time.

At the state level, there is some reason for optimism. The rationale of federal tax reform was the lowering of tax rates with the simultaneous elimination of loopholes. The expectation is that the revenue raised will be essentially the same. Most states with an income tax base their calculation of that tax on the federal model but set their rates independently. As a consequence of federal tax reform, many states face the prospect of a windfall revenue gain unless they lower their tax rates. Most states are expected to take a middle position, lowering rates but not enough to completely offset the revenue gain. Higher education, particularly state-supported colleges and universities, should receive a share of these new revenues. On the other hand, state sales taxes will no longer be deductible for federal tax purposes. States that use a sales tax as a major source of revenue will find increasing resistance from their taxpayers and erosion of taxpayer willingness to fund higher education and other state activities.

Endowment Income. There are a few changes in the new tax law that affect endowment income. The law more rigidly defines reporting requirements for nonprofit organizations and establishes new penalties for reporting violations. In addition, there are rumblings from several corners that perhaps endowment income should be subject to tax. Although these rumblings are not very loud, they are frightening in their implications for the future of higher education finance. Specifically, such a tax would immediately increase costs by diverting endowment income funds from institutional use to payment of tax liability.

Higher Education Expenditures and the New Tax Law

The impact of tax reform on higher education expenditures is not as severe as its impact on revenues. Nevertheless, there are some significant effects in the areas of employee benefits and compliance costs.

Deferred Compensation and Retirement Benefits. The new law makes significant changes in retirement benefits. Beginning in 1987, there are new limits on existing 401(k) (cash or deferral) plans, 403(b) (tax-sheltered annuity) programs, and on other deferred compensation arrangements.

Under the new law, 401(k) plans will not be available to any tax-exempt organizations unless the plans were adopted before July 2, 1986. An employee will be limited to a maximum of $7,000 annual contribution for all existing 401(k) plans in which he participates. This limit will be adjusted for increases in the consumer price index beginning in 1988.

For elective deferral 403(b) plans, the law imposes an annual contribution limit of $9,500. When the limit on contribution to 401(k) plans reaches $9,500, the 403(b) limit will be adjusted in the same manner so that the limits of the two plans will be the same in the future.

The maximum amount that may be deferred each year under a nonqualified deferred compensation arrangement is the lesser of $7,500 or one-third of an individual's compensation. The arrangement for deferral must be made before the compensation is earned, usually at the beginning of the tax year. These limits also apply to nonqualified supplemental retirement programs.

It is important to note that the maximum limits on deferred compensation do not apply to deferrals made under arrangements that were in effect before August 16, 1986, and that called for fixed deferrals or deferrals determined according to a fixed formula.

Nondiscrimination Rules. Nondiscrimination is avowedly an important precept of our colleges and universities. But the standard has generally been one of race, religion, or gender. Now higher education will be held to a complex quantitative accounting for nondiscrimination against lower-paid employees. The consequences may be no less wrenching and costly than for previous discrimination areas.

The new tax law has modified the nondiscrimination rules for 401(k) plans. Discrimination here refers to any differences between ordinary and highly compensated employees. A highly compensated employee is one who (1) earns more than $75,000 per year, (2) earns more than $50,000 per year and is in the top 20 percent of employees by pay, or (3) earns more than $45,000 and is an officer of the corporation. An institution may not have less than three officers, and the new law limits the number of officers to the lesser of 10 percent of employees or fifty.

The average deferral percentage (ADP) of eligible highly compensated employees cannot exceed the greater of (1) 1.25 times the ADP of other eligible employees or (2) 2.0 times the ADP of other eligible employees but not more than 2 percentage points greater than the ADP of other eligible employees.

Beginning in 1989, all qualified programs, including 403(b) and 401(k) plans, will be required to meet new coverage and nondiscrimination requirements.

1. The plan must benefit at least 70 percent of all non-highly compensated employees, or
2. The plan must benefit a percentage of non-highly compensated employees that is at least 70 percent of those highly compensated employees who benefit, or
3. The plan must satisfy a fair cross-section test and provide benefits for non-highly compensated employees that are on average at least 70 percent of the average benefit for all highly compensated employees.

Some employees may be excluded from the coverage test: (1) employees who are covered by a collective bargaining agreement, (2) employees who work less than 17.5 hours per week, (3) employees under twenty-one years of age, (4) students working less than twenty hours per week, and (5) others excluded for specified reasons.

In 1989, all tax-favored retirement plans will be subject to the new uniform distribution requirements. New withdrawal restrictions provide that withdrawals prior to age fifty-nine and a half will be permitted only on account of death, disability, separation of service, or financial hardship, and will be subject to a 10 percent penalty if not on account of death or disability. There are certain exceptions to the 10 percent penalty, including the situation where the distribution is rolled over into an IRA. However, distributions must begin when an individual reaches age seventy and a half, or else an excise tax of 50 percent of the minimum required distribution will be imposed.

Catch-Up Provision. Effective in 1987, an employee with fifteen or more years or service may make 403(b) elective deferral catch-up contributions that exceed the $9,500 limit above, provided they do not violate the Section 415 limits and maximum exclusion allowances that remain in effect. The maximum catch-up contribution is $3,000 per year and $15,000 in aggregate. However, the aggregate catch-up contribution may not exceed $5,000 times the years of service and offset by aggregate 401(k) and 403(b) deferrals to date.

Faculty Housing. For faculty housing on or near the campus to be tax-exempt to a faculty member, the annual rent paid for the housing must be 5 percent or more of the appraised value of the property (the appraisal must be performed by an independent qualified appraiser) or must be demonstrably the fair rental value in the area. If the faculty member is not charged a rental fee, the fair market rental value is taxable to the faculty member.

This standard will be probably be applied using state or local tax assessments as an indication of value. In most areas, these values are somewhat below fair market value. In addition, many institutions house faculty in property that has never been assessed for tax purposes. The need for immediate assessment highlights the costs associated with compliance.

Compliance Costs. The Tax Reform Act of 1986 is likely to increase the tax compliance burden of most institutions of higher education and their patrons by requiring additional data gathering and reporting of information. Among the most significant burdens, in addition to the probable reporting on scholarships, prizes, and awards, are the following:

1. Institutions must dedicate resources to evaluating charitable gifts and examining their acceptance criteria.
2. Unrelated business income estimates must be made and paid quarterly.
3. Institutions must disseminate information to their employees regarding changes in benefit programs that may affect their ability to defer compensation.
4. The new law requires that all tax-exempt interest received must be shown on tax returns, and thus this interest must be reported by issuing institutions.
5. For international students with scholarships, universities will have to institute withholding at a flat 14 percent rate on taxable scholarship amounts. This provision will not ordinarily be overridden by existing tax treaties because the normal treaty provision is to exclude from U.S. tax amounts received by foreign students from abroad but to tax funds received from U.S. sources.

Conclusions

Most Americans applaud the new tax law as it attempts to simplify our system of income tax collection and to reduce the degree to which tax incentives distort economic behavior. The authors join with others in praise of the new law and do not intend the explanation of these changes as an indictment of the overall effect. Nevertheless, higher education, along with other nonprofit activities, is widely perceived as a publicly useful enterprise and was often the beneficiary of incentives that have now been reduced or eliminated. Consequently, this recounting of effects of the Internal Revenue Code of 1986 on colleges and universities is, more often than not, a negative one.

The Tax Reform Act of 1986 creates a number of financial challenges for American colleges and universities. Most major sources of revenue—tuition (including financial aid), contributions, borrowing—are impaired. Meanwhile, the cost of some expenditures—most notably benefits and deferred compensation—are likely to increase. Financing higher education after tax reform will require surmounting new obstacles while taking advantage of opportunities that still exist—such as corporate contributions of equipment and R & E credits.

Gail Franck is a research associate of the Forum for Financing College Alternatives.

Richard E. Anderson is chairman of the Department of Higher and Adult Education at Teachers College, Columbia University, and codirector of the Forum for College Financing Alternatives.

Clark Bernard is a partner and chairman of the National Higher Education Practice of Coopers & Lybrand.

The rapid deterioration of plant and equipment in higher education institutions necessitates quick action by colleges to assess capital needs.

Capital Needs in Higher Education

Harvey H. Kaiser

Assessing capital needs in higher education is complex. Not only the capital requirements for improving facility conditions and making plant improvements must be determined but also the methods of financing. Such a broad discussion is beyond the scope of this chapter, which focuses on capital needs arising from deterioration or obsolescence of existing facilities and new construction.

There are two purposes for determining capital needs. First, the institutional resource requirements for capital budgeting and planning purposes must be established. Without a needs assessment, the individual college or university will suffer from unplanned cash flow and excessive burdens in operating budgets and will continue tolerance of deteriorating physical plants and inadequate equipment. This may be the result of inadequately funded, but required, construction projects, land acquisitions, equipment purchases, or untimely debt.

The second purpose of estimating capital needs is to guide public and private sources of higher education funding. Public sources include both federal and state grants and subsidized loans. In this context, private sources refer to bonds placed by private institutions or through the states acting as agents for either public or private institutions. Without effective guides for public and private funding sources, the shortfall in funding from traditional sources—operating budgets, gifts, and grants—will not be offset.

Several signs illustrate the increasing demands for higher education physical plant funds. Many institutions are announcing major capital campaigns with significant components for plant development, in addition to endowments and unrestricted gifts to augment annual operating budgets. Some campaigns even seek in the hundreds of millions of dollars.

In addition to campus-based initiatives, state governments are increasingly interested in campus conditions. Concerns about the deteriorating physical plants have awakened elected representatives to the perilous conditions on both public and private campuses. Deferred maintenance, relatively unnoticed until a decade ago, has now begun to prompt action. To reduce deferred maintenance, individual campuses have surveyed needs and acquired funds either through internal sources or gifts and grants. Some enlightened state legislatures have responded to well-presented cases of needs or demanded specific data to justify special appropriations. But much more funding is required to reduce the accumulated plant deterioration.

Decay in physical plant and obsolescence in research facilities and equipment are also drawing the attention of the White House and Congress. A 1980 study of scientific instrumentation needs of research universities prepared by the Association of American Universities for the National Science Foundation (NSF) highlighted the dire conditions of campus facilities. Comparisons of university and commercial laboratories revealed that the median age of university equipment in 1980 was *twice* that of the commercial laboratories. A NSF (1982) survey of research equipment in computer science, the physical sciences, and engineering reported that 24 percent of the equipment was obsolete and only 16 percent was state of the art. The fifteen-year decline in federal support and the concurrent lack of university funding led to NSF's conclusion that many research facilities were in need of renovation or replacement.

Research facilities and equipment received further public policy attention through Representative Fuqua's Bill "to assist in the revitalizing of the Nation's academic research programs" (H. R. 2823). The Bill proposed a $10 billion expenditure over ten years on a fifty-fifty federal and nonfederal matching basis. Most recently, the White House Science Council on the Health of U.S. Colleges and Universities Report, *A Renewed Partnership* (1986), called for increased federal support for the higher education scientific enterprise. The council also reached (independently of the Fuqua initiative) the same $10 billion figure required in expenditures for research facilities and equipment over the next ten years. In addition, the council encouraged greater industrial involvement in university research activities.

By intensive lobbying of state legislatures, public and private institutions have gained access to public funding under the guise of economic development. The theory is that investing in the strengths of academic programs, particularly in science and technology, can foster synergy through academic, industrial, and governmental cooperation. The lessons of Route 128 outside Boston, Research Triangle Park in North Carolina, and Silicon Valley underscore the prominent role of higher education in developing new technologies that, in turn, spawn industries and employment opportunities. New York State's initiative for Centers of Advanced Technology brought direct grants for programs and equipment that could attract industry to work with campus researchers. Recently announced long-term no-interest loans to Columbia, Cornell, and Syracuse universities of approximately $100 million for science and technology centers are also good examples of state support.

A corollary of assessing renewal and replacement needs is the portrayal of the big picture. A comprehensive overview of campus plant needs, including deferred maintenance with programmatic requirements and enhancement of faculty and student support services, must be developed. Currently, strategic facilities planning that links academic and student life facility requirements with plans to eliminate plant deterioration is emerging. This comprehensive approach is producing capital campaigns and more vigorous lobbying for public policy to provide funding for campus capital needs.

Physical Plant Expenditures and Assets

The annual expenditures for operating, maintaining, and adding to plant summarizes the levels of resources dedicated by higher education to its plant assets. How much is expended on operations and maintenance has a direct effect on the conditions of campus facilities. The amounts spent on plant additions represent capitalized investments to replace obsolete facilities, meet new program requirements, and enhance the quality of campus life. An analysis of past decisions allocating current and plant funds offers some insights into future capital needs.

Current fund education and general expenditures for operation and maintenance of plant include all expenditures for services and maintenance related to grounds and facilities. The National Association of College and University Business Officers defines these as costs for physical plant administration, building maintenance, custodial services, utilities, landscape and grounds maintenance, and major repairs and renovations. The last category, major repairs and renovations, often creates confusion by including work more appropriately classified as capitalized renewal and replacement work.

In reviewing plant operations and maintenance expenditures in the last decade, one might expect some increases that reflect the following factors: increasing enrollments causing additional wear and tear on facilities; higher required levels of maintenance for more technologically sophisticated buildings; drastically increased utility costs; and inflationary effects on maintenance costs for personnel, materials, and services exceeding rises in the Consumer Price Index. The accumulation of plant improvement costs for the older campus buildings contributes to demands for additional plant operations and maintenance.

Despite these demands, the portions of funds for operations and maintenance remained almost constant from fiscal year 1975 to 1984. Fluctuations were less than 1 percent, ranging from 10 to 11 percent of total education and general expenditures for operations and maintenance. The tentative conclusion is that the unfunded needs of deferred maintenance will continue to grow.

By examining the book value of plant additions for buildings and equipment, we can get an indication of levels of plant fund expenditures for renewals and replacements and new construction. From 1970 to 1983, book value for buildings more than doubled. Converting the annual additions to 1983–84 constant dollars using the Boeckh Construction Index presents a more accurate picture of trends in annual plant additions. From $7.8 billion in 1970–71, plant additions declined to $3.7 billion in 1983–84. In constant dollars per student, expenditures for new construction dropped from a peak of $577 in 1967 to $120 per student in 1983.

An overbuilding of higher education in the 1960s ended in the 1970s with stable or declining enrollments. However, the drastic decline in plant additions for building, combined with near-level operations and maintenance expenditures, suggests an increase in deferred maintenance and a pent-up demand for upgrading and renovations and new construction.

Book value increases from 1970 to 1983 also showed a steady increase for new equipment and replacements, rising from $800 million to $2.7 billion. In constant dollars, additions for equipment were relatively level until 1980. As a result of increased federal aid for higher education equipment purchases, additions to equipment value have risen dramatically. With trends in all prices up sharply, future equipment purchases should buy less than in the past.

Determining Capital Needs

How much is needed to meet the capital requirements for higher education's physical plant? Seeking the answer is an elusive quest. The frustrating response is that in the national aggregate there is no reliable measure. But by assessing historic data and anecdotal information, some general estimates can be prepared. However, new construction to meet programmatic requests or enhancements to the quality of campus life remains unquantifiable.

Ideally, the summary of individual campus resource needs for buildings, grounds, utilities, and equipment would provide aggregates for system, state, or national comparisons. Unfortunately, there is no uniformity in the instruments for collecting such data, and this deficiency prevents the compilations necessary for presenting a convincing public policy picture.

The information gap existing at the campus level also prevents reliable intercampus comparisons of need. Many campuses continue to make capital budget decisions in the traditional manner: High priority programmatic requirements struggle to the surface along with the most pressing renewal or deferred maintenance priorities. Missing is any systematic audit of facility conditions or an evaluation process for determining long-range priorities.

A promising source of capital needs information has resulted from demands of governing boards and state legislators for justifications for funding requests. Unlike the traditional compilation of line item requests for renovations or plant additions, many campuses now make detailed surveys of plant conditions and justifications of facilities before introducing fund-raising campaigns or presenting requests to governing boards or legislators. This more thorough preparation has produced new streams of funding for deferred maintenance and new facilities. Even when only funding needs on a partial basis, the initial responses have been encouraging.

The lack of comprehensive data on existing conditions and anticipated needs prevents a clear set of conclusions of resource requirements. This frustration can be overcome partially by reviewing available data and anecdotal information on existing conditions. Relationships between plant replacement, values, and estimated costs for correcting existing conditions provide ranges of need for overall capital requirements.

The last national survey of the condition of higher education facilities was prepared in the fall of 1974. It was then reported that approximately 20 percent of campus facilities were in unsatisfactory condition. Some recent statewide and campus surveys of facility conditions are consistent with that ratio.

1. *North Carolina.* A 1982 facilities and inventory study of public and private institutions with 72 million gross square feet reported 17.4 percent of space in an unsatisfactory condition. The estimated cost of restoring the space to a satisfactory condition was $301.6 million.
2. *University of California System.* A detailed survey in 1983 of 60 million square feet had a capital maintenance backlog of approximately $2 billion at $33.60 per square foot.
3. *Texas.* A 1982 survey of twenty-five institutions of the College and University System Coordinating Board (which excludes the University of Texas and Texas A. & M.) evaluated conditions of educational and general facilities ten years and older. Total costs of renewals and replacements for 21.3 million square feet was estimated at $301 million.

4. *Indiana.* A 1983 survey of the Indiana Commission for Higher Education's seventy-eight campuses totaling 33.6 million gross square feet reported 24 percent of space in unsatisfactory condition. Total replacement value was $3.34 billion.
5. *University of Maryland.* In 1985 a report was presented to the Maryland board of regents for the eight campuses of the University of Maryland. Critical capital needs were defined for a five-year period totaling $555.5 million: $224.1 million to correct deteriorated facility conditions and $331.4 million for new facilities. The 1986 allocation for deferred maintenance was $2.5 million, despite an estimated annual renewal need of $22.5 million.
6. *New York.* A 1982 survey of 196 million gross square feet reported 20 percent of the space in unsatisfactory condition.

Similar surveys in Kansas, Iowa, and Arkansas reported approximately 10 to 15 percent of all facilities required renewal or replacement. Two private institutions provide supportive data on the magnitude of costs for renewal and replacement. Columbia University prepared a detailed survey of conditions in 1984 for 7.11 million gross square feet of space. The estimated capital maintenance backlog was $247 million at $34 per gross square foot. Syracuse University conducted an intensive campaign to eliminate deferred maintenance beginning in 1972 for 7.1 million gross square feet that eventually cost over $170 million. Adjusting these costs to 1984 dollars produces a total similar to Columbia University's projections.

There are two approaches for determining the major repairs and upgrading and renovation components of capital needs. The most thorough approach is a campus-based audit of existing conditions of buildings, grounds, utilities, and equipment. An alternate method is to use life-cycle analyses in lieu of actual amounts comprising the backlog of deferred maintenance. By factoring the age and replacement cost of building components, a renewal and replacement allowance can be budgeted to offset facility aging each year. Empirical studies have produced ranges of 1.5 to 3 percent of plant replacement value as appropriate levels of annual funding for renewal and replacement.

Added to annual funding are costs to correct existing deferred maintenance. The 20 percent level of unsatisfactory conditions is a reasonable assumption based on the historical data and selected examples. Using this assumption, higher education's 1983–84 total building replacement value of $181 billion would require $36.3 billion to correct deferred maintenance. Adding equipment replacement value brings the total to over $200 billion and a deferred maintenance funding requirement of $40 to $50 billion.

At a modest inflation rate of 3 percent, an annual commitment of between $4 and $5 billion is required nationally to eliminate deferred maintenance. In addition, a minimum of 1.5 percent of total replacement value of buildings and equipment requires almost $3 billion a year for

For a campus with $300 million in replacement value for buildings and equipment, this translates into $60 million for deferred maintenance and $4.5 million a year for facility renewal. Omitted are the projections for capital additions.

How much of the $3.7 billion spent on campus plant additions in 1983-84 was for major repairs, upgrading and renovations, or new construction is unclear. However, the ubiquitous reports of deterioration, aging facilities, and obsolete equipment suggest unmet capital needs much higher than the amount spent in that year.

An important principle for campus decision makers and higher education policy makers to remember is that a one-time elimination of current renewal and replacement priorities does not solve the problem. As campus facilities continue to deteriorate and become obsolete, an annual allocation for renewal and replacement is necessary to prevent further accumulation of deferred maintenance. Establishing an appropriate level of annual funding in the beginning of a facility program may have to include catch-up costs. As needs are reduced to manageable proportions, the operating budget can accommodate priorities as they are identified. The end result is a program that should maintain campus facilities in good repair so they are functionally adequate for instruction, research, campus life, and community service.

Research Facilities and Equipment

The reports on physical plant deterioration were of special interest to those concerned about the health of the higher education research enterprise. Where 60 percent of the nation's basic research is conducted at universities, the condition of the supporting infrastructure for science and technology has raised alarms. The NSF reports (1985) that growing costs of conducting research have led to diversion of funds from facilities and equipment maintenance and improvements to the support of research projects. Some facilities, for example, require renovation for compliance with new regulatory standards for health and safety, handling of dangerous materials, and hazardous waste disposal. In some cases, facilities need to be constructed to keep pace with theoretical advances; computer facilities are a noteworthy example.

Deterioration in physical plant, the need for growth in science and technology, and a strong academic research capability have prompted Congress to act. To overcome the lack of quantitative information and to provide a basis for an informed assessment of academic research facility needs, Congress directed the National Science Foundation to assess research facility needs in higher education. NSF has just completed a baseline survey of all doctorate-granting institutions that provides previously unavailable data on this important part of higher education's capital needs. (There is no 1987 survey; one is mandated by Congress for 1988.)

The NSF study (1986), conducted by a mail survey and telephone canvass of research administrators and academic officers, covered institutions accounting for 83 percent of total research and development expenditures at universities and medical schools in 1984. A more comprehensive national survey of science and engineering research facility needs is to be prepared for 1988. Although the NSF sample included only the most active institutions, the estimates of need and opinions on future capital requirements are useful.

The study found that the estimated completion cost of all facilities-related work in academic year 1985–86 at doctorate-granting institutions was $1.7 billion, compared to total research and development costs of about $9.3 billion. Completion costs for facilities-related work planned over the period 1986–91 is estimated to be $5.8 billion. Considering the three- to five-year period for delivery of projects, these estimates can be considered as reliable values for future construction commitments.

The distribution of current construction expenditures is relatively consistent across all universities, with nearly seventy-eight cents of each dollar going to build new facilities, sixteen cents to upgrading, and about six cents to major repairs. Average institutional expenditures for work in progress were approximately $14 million for new construction, $2.9 million for upgrading, and $1 million for major repairs.

The distribution of types of projects and costs will shift for work planned between 1986 and 1991. New construction will use sixty-six cents of each dollar, twenty-three cents will go to upgrading, and eleven cents to major repairs. Estimates of planned work for average institutional expenditures will rise to $32.5 million for new construction, $11.2 million for upgrading, and $5.4 million for major repairs. Over 80 percent of the universities plan to construct new research facilities, about 84 percent plan upgrading or renovations in the next five years, and just over three-fourths plan major repairs in the same period.

Funding for work in progress and planned work for facility repairs, upgrading, and construction were allocated to four sources in the survey: the federal government, the state budget (excluding the university's normal allocation for operating budget), tax-exempt bonds, and private donations or endowments. As would be expected, data comparisons show that public universities rely more on state funds, and private universities rely more on donations or earnings from endowment yields. State budgets provided at least half of the public institution's financing of facility expenditures, and private institutions receive on average over one-third of their funds from endowments.

For 1985–86, state governments accounted for the highest percentage (40 percent) of the new construction funds, tax-exempt bonds furnished 30 percent of new construction costs, and private donations 14 percent. The proportion of funds obtained from federal sources (10 percent) was about the same for new construction as for repairs and upgrading or renovation.

State governments and tax-exempt bonds each provided almost one-third of the costs for upgrading and renovations in progress. Somewhat less than a quarter of these costs, as well as those of major repairs, were financed by private donations. State governments provided half of the funds for major repairs.

Thirty-five percent of new construction in progress at private institutions was financed with federal funds, compared to less than 1 percent at public institutions. Private universities also received 29 percent of their new construction funds from private donations and endowment earnings; public universities received only 9 percent from that source. The major sources of funds for new construction at public universities were state governments (53 percent) and tax-exempt bonds (35 percent).

All universities anticipate less federal money for new construction in the next five years. Private sources and, to a lesser extent, state government are expected to compensate for decreases in federal money. Universities also plan to use more tax-exempt bonds to finance repairs. However, new tax limitations on the amount of debt issued by private schools may reduce this opportunity.

Traditional sources are expected to provide larger shares of the costs of planned new construction at both public and private institutions. Over 60 percent of the costs at public universities will be supplied by state governments; over 40 percent of the costs at private universities should come from donations and endowment earnings. When compared to work in progress, private universities will generally rely more on tax-exempt bonds to finance planned work, while public universities will rely less on that source.

The NSF survey is valuable as an example for gathering data on a rapid response basis for public policy guidance. Selectivity in sampling and an understanding of qualifications needed to analyze the data should not cloud the importance of the breakthrough in gathering facility needs information at the national level represented by this survey. Although only a subset of overall national facility needs, the conclusions drawn from the survey of costs of work underway and planned for the next five years and future funding sources offer insights on overall higher education capital needs.

Conclusions

Two groups need information on the capital needs of higher education: The state and federal governments require information for public policy guidance, and each campus must formulate its own plans. The difficulty of assessing resource requirements for campus buildings, grounds, utilities, and equipment is compounded by the lack of quantitative information about deteriorating facilities and equipment and projections of plant additions.

Resolving the lack of information and policies for meeting higher education capital needs requires specific plans of action at campus and national levels. A plan of action must address several fundamental questions: What is the extent of capital renewal and replacement needs of existing facilities? What are the capital needs for new construction to meet programmatic requirements? What are the most appropriate campus and public policy strategies for obtaining resources to meet capital needs?

An institutional plan of action should include the following points:
1. Enlist presidential leadership to form a campus committee including governing boards, administrators, faculty, students, and alumni.
2. Develop a strategic facilities plan for inventorying existing conditions of buildings, grounds, utilities, and equipment for selection of priorities and for projections of new facility requirements.
3. Establish funding requirements with a capital budget and schedule of projects.
4. Seek resources for creating overall institutional advancement programs incorporating a broad base of support within the campus community and presentation of a case statement including funding needs to private donors, corporations and foundations, and government agencies.

The magnitude of higher education capital needs requires concerted action at the national level. Although each college and university needs an institutional plan of action, a national plan of action requires involvement of the appropriate higher education associations representing trustees and administrators, government officials, legislators, private sector representatives, and market funding sources.

A coalition of education, government, and business leaders could elicit public support, influence public policy, and encourage increased action at campus, state, and national levels. These broad goals could be accomplished by a national survey containing the following components:
1. Prepare a national inventory of existing conditions and projected facility requirements.
2. Determine funding requirements for major repairs, upgrading and renovations, and new construction.
3. Disseminate findings to legislative bodies, government agencies, higher education associations, and national media.
4. Recommend funding strategies for public policies and private funding markets.

The White House Science Council Panel on the Health of U.S. Colleges and Universities (1986) stated that:

> America has a unique dependence upon its colleges and universities both for new knowledge and for young minds to be

trained to use this knowledge in innovative ways; the excellence of our colleges and universities has been a cornerstone of our economic well-being, our national security, and the health and quality of life of our citizens. But . . . the strength and excellence of this higher education enterprise is at a transition point, and can no longer be taken for granted.

If institutions are to fulfill their missions now and in the coming decades, resources for capital needs must be resolved.

References

Association of American Universities. *The Scientific Instrumentation Needs of Research Universities.* Washington, D.C.: Association of American Universities, 1980.

Executive Office of the President. *A Renewed Policy.* A Report of the White House Science Council on the Health of U.S. Colleges and Universities to the Office of Science and Technology Policy. Washington, D.C.: Government Printing Office, 1986.

National Science Foundation. *National Survey of Academic Research Instruments and Instrumentation Needs.* Washington, D.C.: National Science Foundation, 1982.

National Science Foundation. *Science Indicators: The 1985 Report.* Washington, D.C.: National Science Foundation, 1985.

National Science Foundation. *Science and Engineering Research Facilities at Doctorate-Granting Institutions.* Washington, D.C.: National Science Foundation, 1986.

Harvey H. Kaiser is senior vice-president at Syracuse University, with primary responsibility for facilities management.

The tax-exempt bond market continues to be unsettled, but many issues have been resolved by the Tax Reform Act of 1986.

Tax Reform and the Bond Market

David C. Clapp

During the past ten years, sophisticated new techniques and dramatic changes in capital markets have opened up new and complex ways of obtaining capital funds. Colleges and universities are able to use these methods, providing the institutions are credit worthy and have some reasonable market access. In fact, even at this moment new developments should provide assistance to higher education as it seeks to rebuild infrastructure and provide desperately needed research facilities.

Unfortunately, another new development limits the ability of colleges and universities to use these new techniques. The Tax Reform Act of 1986 will have a generally negative impact on financing with tax-exempt securities. Perhaps the *Wall Street Journal*'s (1986) summary of the Act said it best: "Bond people were hit coming and going in the new tax bill. Issuers will be limited in the amount of bonds they could offer; purchasers would have to pay taxes on many of these generally exempt instruments." The changes in the tax law range from very narrow technical adjustments to sweeping new limits applicable to all issuers. And some of the new restrictions are directly aimed at colleges and universities.

Government Use and Private Activity Bonds

Bonds of states and political subdivisions are generally considered either governmental use bonds or private activity bonds. Governmental use bonds are usually exempt from federal income tax, but private activity bonds are subject to tax unless they fit into one of a number of categories designated qualified private activity bonds. Qualified private activity bonds are subject to more severe limitations than governmental use bonds in establishing and maintaining their tax exemption, except for qualified 501(c)(3) bonds. Qualified 501(c)(3) bonds, although designated qualified private activity bonds, are, in many cases, exempted from the tests applicable to private activity bonds and treated more like governmental use bonds.

In the Tax Reform Act of 1986, tests to distinguish between governmental use bonds and private activity bonds have been changed. Rather than the 25 percent trade or business test and the 25 percent security interest test in the old law, there is now a 10 percent trade or business test and a 10 percent security interest test. Consequently, the new law permits considerably less private involvement in public projects financed with tax-exempt bonds.

Perhaps an example will make the above percentage test clearer. A state college may wish to fund the construction of a dormitory with debt. If the dormitories include a cafeteria run by a private contractor, and cafeteria revenues exceed 10 percent of dormitory revenues, the bonds issued to finance the dormitory are probably not eligible for tax-exempt status. Even more worrisome is that the loss of tax-exempt status can be made retroactive. If at any time subsequent to the issuance of the bonds there is significant private activity in the buildings financed with tax-exempt bonds, the bonds may be made taxable as of the date of issuance. The level of private interest is considerably less for tax-exempt debt issued by private colleges and universities.

Public higher education institutions' issues generally fall under the category of governmental use bonds, and private institutions' issues usually are qualified 501(c)(3) bonds. This produces tremendous inequality of treatment between public and private higher education institutions. Public institutions are allowed virtually unlimited access to the tax-exempt market (subject only to those restrictions applicable to governmental use bonds, such as rebate of excess arbitrage profits). Private universities are subject to the provisions applicable to qualified 501(c)(3) bonds, which include most significantly an institutional cap on tax-exempt financing of $150 million outstanding at any time.

According to a report issued by the Task Force on Higher Education Finance (1986), such a cap will cause more than twenty-five private universities to lose access to the tax-exempt market. At the same time, public institutions, regardless of volume, will be allowed the financial advantage. Such a restriction is an arbitrary, yet significant, discrimination among schools. With interest rate differentials of as much as 4 percent between taxable and nontaxable debt instruments, a competitive advantage could result for public institutions. This is a double blow to private institutions, which already suffer from the weakening of the charitable contributions deduction. Many private institutions may have to forgo much needed maintenance and rehabilitation for their significantly older campuses. The cap also ignores the fact that, although educational institutional needs for capital are relatively small, they are vital to the educational system in the United States and should not be denied complete tax-exempt status.

The average volume of debt issued for 501(c)(3) organizations in 1983, 1984, and 1985 of $14.2 billion will be cut to approximately $6.3 billion, based on figures from reports of the Task Force on Higher Educationa Finance (1986).

Certain state or local governmental universities and hospitals (including certain public benefit corporations) also have been classified as tax exempt under Section 501(c)(3). To the extent that such an entity is a governmental unit or an agency or instrumentality of a governmental unit (as determined under present law), bonds for the entity would be treated as governmental bonds rather than as qualified 501(c)(3) bonds.

Furthermore, certain facilities eligible for financing with qualified 501(c)(3) bonds may comprise part of a larger facility otherwise ineligible for such financing, or portions of a section 501(c)(3) organization facility may be used for activities of persons other than section 501(c)(3) organizations or governmental units. The Treasury Department may adopt rules for allocating the costs of such mixed-use facilities (including common elements) according to any reasonable method that reflects the proportionate benefit to be derived by the various users of the facility. Only the portions of such mixed-use facilities owned and used by section 501(c)(3) organizations may be financed with tax-exempt bonds.

Five Percent Private Activity Limit and Costs of Issuance

Another provision of the new tax law that affects both private and public institutions of higher education is the 5 percent rule. This rule states that no more than 5 percent of the proceeds of an issue may be used for trade or business with a nongovernmental entity. Should the limit be exceeded, the bonds will be deemed taxable retroactive to the date of issue. In addition, all costs of issuance must be taken from that same 5 percent, and those costs may not exceed 2 percent. Thus, the percentage available for private activity will be even less than 5 percent. Additionally, the 2 percent cost of issuance may prove very difficult for issuers with smaller projects. This provision will obviously affect the way universities do business, particularly relating to food services, financial aid services, and research. Insurance premiums and letter of credit fees may, however, be deemed interest expense rather than cost of issuance.

This limitation on private use poses special problems for research universities that enter into cooperative research agreements with for-profit organizations. State and other governmental universities are similarly restricted, but at the higher 10 percent exclusion.

There is no restriction on using bond-financed property to perform general (as opposed to product development) research supported by a for-profit organization as part of a cooperative research arrangement. Similarly, any cooperative research agreement that provides that the sponsoring organization have access to the resulting technology on the same basis as any third party should not jeopardize tax-exempt status. Thus, a cooperative research agreement that provides a license of any resulting technology at a royalty rate fixed in advance of the performance of the research could constitute such a trade or business use. However, an agreement with only a first right of refusal (at a competitive price) for the sponsoring person would probably not constitute such a use. This raises the issue of whether business-sponsored research projects that are not purely for charity will be cost effective for the business.

Arbitrage Requirements and Reserve Restrictions

Tax-exempt debt pays interest at several percentage points below taxable debt. Obviously, a dollar of tax-free income is worth more than a dollar subject to federal taxes, and the bond market acknowledges the difference in value between the two forms of debt. But agencies of state and local government, as well as 501(c)(3) organizations, essentially pay no taxes. Consequently, there is an opportunity for issuers of tax-exempt debt to make a short-term profit by reinvesting proceeds of the low interest tax-exempt issue in higher interest taxable issues until such time as the funds are needed. This is called arbitrage income. Previous revisions of the tax code restricted the opportunities for arbitrage income; the Tax Reform Act of 1986 has practically eliminated them.

For example, arbitrage requirements, including rebate of arbitrage profits previously applicable only to industrial development bonds, will now apply to all tax-exempt bonds, including governmental use bonds. Thus, private and public higher education institutions will not be able to retain any investment earnings on bond proceeds in excess of the bond yield. (This provision excludes cost of issuance, which generally would make the bond yield and permissible investment rate higher.) Earnings must be calculated each year, and excess earnings must be rebated every five years. Furthermore, the minor portion of proceeds that may be invested at an unrestricted yield would be reduced from the present 15 percent (which includes a required reserve) to the lesser of 5 percent of bond proceeds or $100,000 (not including a reserve fund). A reserve fund is generally limited to 10 percent of proceeds unless the reserve is funded by nonbond issue proceeds, in which case those funds do not count against the 10 percent limit. The reserve fund is, nevertheless, subject to the same arbitrage requirements. Even for a temporary period of three years, arbitrage profits must be rebated; the temporary period rules only provide a respite for the administrative burdens of dealing with restricted yield investments.

Refundings

Interest rates rise and fall in line with market forces. If, after debt is issued, interest rates should fall significantly, the issuer may wish to refinance the old debt at a lower rate. New debt issued to retire old debt before it is due is called an advance refunding.

The new tax law defines and restricts the types and number of permissible advance refundings. In general, pre-1986 bonds may be refunded twice and post-1986 bonds may be refunded only once. Unless already previously refunded, there are a number of other structural restrictions, including rules for calling bonds, temporary periods, and issuance expense.

The average maturity of bonds cannot exceed 120 percent of the average reasonably expected economic life of the assets financed, and 501(c)(3) bonds will have to be approved by an elected public official after a public hearing.

Financing Considerations in the New Tax Era

It is clear that the tax law will severely restrict the issuance of debt by private educational institutions and hamper the cost effectiveness of debt for governmental public institutions. Educational institutions will need to reassess their capital requirements very carefully and scrutinize the costs and benefits of financing projects with particular financing techniques. If, for example, a private institution has more than $150 million of debt outstanding, it will need to evaluate whether taxable debt financing of a project is more desirable and/or economical than a lease or if the taxable financing complements the outstanding tax-exempt financings. For a public institution wishing to engage in a private trade or business (privatization), such private involvement will have to be weighed against loss of tax-exempt status. Taxable financing methods, however, will be useful only to the extent that they are necessary and appropriate under the circumstances.

For example, if an issuer should determine that commercial paper is the financing vehicle it wants to utilize, it is still more likely that the issuer will issue Tax-Exempt Commercial Paper rather than taxable (if issuer can) because the issuer may be able to invest in longer tax-exempts such as Variable Rate Demand Notes (VRDNs) and avoid any negative

negative cost of carrying (net of issuance expense). But any financing plan will have to incorporate the use of techniques that offset the incremental cost of a taxable financing. And the administrative burden of investing so as to comply with the rebate requirements will be significant.

Miscellaneous Tax-Exempt Items

Some secondary concerns of the new tax law as it affects tax-exempt bond issues are discussed in this section.

Alternative Minimum Tax. Neither governmental education bond issues nor qualified 501(c)(3) institutions should be subject to the corporate or individual alternative minimum tax (AMT). This is good news because debt that is subject to AMT must offer a higher interest rate to attract investors.

Cost of Carry. The new tax law eliminates the 80 percent deduction for interest expenses incurred by financial institutions to purchase or carry tax-exempt bonds acquired after August 1986, although there is an exception for bonds issued by a small issuer that does not issue more than $10 million a year. This provision will raise the cost of issuance and dilute the market for tax-exempt debt.

Credit Considerations. It is not clear yet what impact the tax law will have on the credit-worthiness of educational issuers. The extent to which institutions issue less debt is a two-edged sword. On the one hand, less debt is better. However, rating agencies and investors will not have positive perceptions of an institution that is unable to make infrastructure improvements or manage its finances efficiently. The challenge to manage and finance higher educational institutions effectively will only increase.

Conclusion—After Tax Reform

Recent tax reform has created an uproar as it applies to tax-exempt bonds. Whatever may be the virtues of tax reform, and there are many, issuers of bonds have been restricted to a greater extent than ever before. In general, it was the intent of both the Treasury Department and the Joint Committee on Taxation to lower the total volume of tax-exempt bonds that, they argue, costs the U.S. Treasury money. Although the revenue gains from revising the bond rules were modest, even by the Joint Tax Committee's own calculations, the reforms were pushed through by the committee. One major device used to do so included specific restrictions, on a state-by-state basis, of the amount of bonds that could be issued for certain purposes. The other device, as mentioned earlier, was to disallow certain benefits that might be derived from arbitrage and certain kinds of bond refundings.

The news is not very good for colleges and universities classified as

501(c)(3). Such institutions may not have more than $150 million of tax-exempt debt, including amounts outstanding prior to the passage of the law. It also will not generally be permissible to earn any arbitrage on invested funds. Although higher education institutions may refund debt in the future, there are significant restrictions on using advance refundings. Advance refundings, which previously could occur at any time, were extremely useful for lowering interest rates when the market changed and in revising issuing documents to eliminate overly restrictive covenants or to include state-of-the-art security provisions.

Also disturbingly, 501(c)(3) bonds have for the first time been classified in the code as private activity bonds. This category had been previously reserved for industrial revenue bonds and other bonds that are deemed to benefit a private entity or individual or that are to be paid by such an entity or individual. The obvious problem is that while 501(c)(3) institutions are private, they are also not-for-profit, and the new tax law lumps them with for-profit entities for certain bond purposes. It is likely, now that the classification is in place, that these institutions will be vulnerable to other restrictions as Congress passes future amendments to the tax laws.

Most worrisome among these amendments would be inclusion of 501(c)(3) organizations in the state-by-state per capita volume caps. Their inclusion had been considered in the early stages of tax reform but dropped at the last minute. These new caps, which amount to the lesser of $75 per capita or $200 million, could make it almost impossible for private independent institutions to use tax-exempt bonds, since they would be competing for cap authorization with issuers of bonds for voluntary hospitals, housing, and all forms of industrial revenue bonds.

Happily, public institutions are still classified as governmental use facilities in the law. This is, of course, because they are publicly owned. But it is bewildering that Congress does not also accept the essential use purpose associated with the invaluable and historic role of independent higher education in this country.

A positive development to come out of the congressional session was the creation of the College Construction Loan Insurance Association, an independent corporation to be owned jointly by the federal government, higher education institutions, Sallie Mae, and the general public. The new insurer is authorized to insure and reissue college and university loans, to give letters of credit, and to make direct loans. The corporation is mandated to do a significant percentage of its business with institutions with weaker credit ratings. This should provide assistance to a large number of institutions that at present, and historically, have had little or no capital market access. At the same time, the new corporation, which may only operate in the higher education field, should provide needed expansion to the capacity now provided by the current major bond insurers (Municipal Bond Insurance Association; American Municipal Bond Assurance Corporation, AMBAC; Financial Guaranty Insurance Corporation; and Bond Investors Guaranty Corporation). If college loans must be done on a taxable basis, the new corporation will be very important. Coordination with state agencies and authorities should produce solid financing programs.

Other sources for debt financing will doubtless become available. The foreign market is still relatively untapped. The main trouble with the foreign market until now is that it has required big issues (to get attention) and short amortization. Some other devices, such as tuition fee futures, may begin to find acceptance as time goes on. College and university financings occupy a reasonably good niche in the debt markets. The default and late payment records are excellent, better than statistics for housing and health care. The defaults that have occurred have received attention because of their infrequency. But the higher education coalition should not lose sight of the fact that the environment of capital financing is not as good as it has been in the past. The lack of federal support is documented. The fact that colleges and universities are in a competitive environment at a time when costs are rising faster than the ability to increase revenues is not lost on investors. It seems that financing devices exist but that ability to access those devices is far from certain. Many institutions are already leveraged and, on average, their financing needs do not attract the same attention as larger users. Using credit enhancement, creating pools for financing, and making use of public authorities (in the states where they are available) seem worthy of increased attention. And a louder voice in Washington would appear to be a priority, given the overall treatment afforded higher education by Congress in the recent tax legislation.

References

"For Many Firms, Overhaul Bill Means Higher Taxes, Repeal of Investment Incentives Crafted by Reagan." *Wall Street Journal,* August 18, 1986, p. 10.
Task Force on Higher Education Finance. *Report: March 1986*. Washington, D.C.: Municipal Bond Insurance Association, 1986.

David C. Clapp is a partner at Goldman Sachs & Company and currently heads their public finance practice.

Tax-exempt leasing is emerging as an attractive and practical option for financing equipment and facilities.

Tax-Exempt Leasing for Colleges and Universities

C. Gregory H. Eden

Tax-exempt leases are financing mechanisms used by governments and other specifically enabled entities for acquiring equipment and facilities; funds may be borrowed at tax-exempt interest rates with repayment terms ranging from several months to thirty years. This chapter explores tax-exempt leasing, compares it to other financing mechanisms, and examines its applicability and the variety of structuring options available to public colleges and universities as lessees. The impact of the Tax Reform Act of 1986 and the Act's effect on the future of tax-exempt leasing is also examined.

Public colleges and universities are considered political subdivisions for tax purposes, and this enables them to engage in tax-exempt leasing. Section 103 of the Internal Revenue Code of 1954, as amended, provides the basis for all tax-exempt leasing. A potential lessee is defined as "a State, a Territory, or a possession of the United States, or any political subdivision of the foregoing, or the District of Columbia." Conversely, private colleges and universities do not constitute political subdivisions. Hence, they can only avail themselves of tax-exempt lease opportunities by engaging the services of a public authority duly constituted by state legislation. Although all states now possess such authorities, variously known as higher education or economic development authorities, the tax-exempt lease process is somewhat more complicated for these private institutions. Typically, they rely on a lease/sublease arrangement in which the tax-exempt authority serves as the initial lessee and sublessor. The authority agrees to obligate itself for repayment of monies due but looks directly to the sublessee private institution for actual payment of amounts due under the lease.

Tax-Exempt Leasing

Tax-exempt leasing, municipal leasing, tax-exempt conditional sale financing, and municipal lease/purchase financing are interchangeable terms. They all describe an alternative financing approach to payment of cash, entering into an operating lease, or issuing of bonds. A tax-exempt lease enables a college or university, as a lessee, to enter into a tax-exempt conditional sale agreement that, by the insertion of certain language, is characterized as a current expense rather than a debt obligation.

The tax-exempt lease is a financing lease, conditional sale contract, or a lease with purchase option. It differs from an operating lease in several respects. First, a tax-exempt lease provides that title to the equipment or facilities transfers to the lessee at either commencement of the lease term or the end of the term of the contract on payment of a nominal consideration. In an operating lease, ownership remains with the lessor, and the lessee is entitled only to the use of the equipment or facilities for the duration of the lease term.

The operating lease also provides for payments without a principal and interest component. Therefore, the lessor, until recently, relied on depreciation as the primary tax benefit when the lessee was a political subdivision. In a tax-exempt lease, however, payments by the lessee include an interest component that is exempt from federal, and frequently state, income taxation based on Section 103 of the Internal Revenue Code.

Tax-exempt leases contrast with other types of tax-exempt obligations by incorporating nonappropriation language to avoid the characterization of debt. Other tax-exempt obligations may be backed by revenues as the full faith and credit of the issuer. Tax-exempt leases rely instead on the lessee's credit rating as well as the essentiality of the equipment or facilities being financed.

Tax Considerations

Most tax-exempt leases are structured as full payout leases or conditional sales. They are designed so that the cash return to the lessor pays for the asset value of the property as well as financing costs.

In order for the interest component to qualify as tax-exempt, the transaction must, as in the case of other obligations such as bonds, conform to the provisions of Section 103(a)(1) of the Internal Revenue Code, which provides that "Gross income does not include interest on (1) the obligation of a State, a Territory, or a possession of the United States, or any political subdivision of any of the foregoing, or of the District of Columbia."

This section of the Code may be applied to leases of equipment and facilities to public colleges and universities and the subsequent offering of these lease obligations to institutional or private investors. Certain general rules must be followed before the interest earned by investors on the obligations can be excluded from gross income for federal income tax purposes.

1. The college or university obligor under the lease must be a political subdivision. In many instances, a governmental body established by statute can qualify as an obligor under Section 103(a)(1).
2. The obligation of the governmental body must be one that is created in the exercise of the governmental body's borrowing power. The obligation can take one of several forms: lease, bond, certificate, or contract. In transactions involving the lease of property to a governmental body, the lease must constitute a sale; that is, an absolute and unconditional obligation to purchase on the part of the governmental body must exist, and the risk of loss must lie with the governmental body.
3. The public college or university must be the primary obligor under the lease. The lessor or his assignee must look solely to the college or university for payment and not to some third party. In the case of a private college or university, the duly constituted state authority must be the primary obligor under the lease. In this event, the authority serves as a lessee and sublessor, with the private college or university captioned as sublessee and accepting all obligations of the authority. The authority thus serves as a conduit to qualify the transaction as a tax-exempt obligation for the private college or university.
4. The obligation must separately set out the amount and interest included in each payment.

If a qualifying college or university enters into an absolute and unconditional purchase agreement (not a true or operating lease) in which it promises to pay interest, that interest payment may be excluded for federal tax purposes from the gross income of the lessor or third party.

Nonappropriation (Fiscal Funding Out)

The insertion of a nonappropriation (also known as a fiscal funding out) provision in the tax-exempt lease eliminates the ongoing dilemma, associated with the multiyear lease with purchase option method, of whether or not indebtedness is incurred by the college or university. Nonappropriation language enables the college or university to avoid lease payment obligations beyond its then-current fiscal period, thereby making the incremental lease payments a current expense of the lessee. Nonappropriation language may vary from jurisdiction to jurisdiction, but typically reads as follows:

> If the Lessee is not allotted funds for the next Fiscal period to continue the leasing of the Equipment and it has not funds for such leasing from other sources, Lessee may terminate this Lease at the end of the then current fiscal period upon forty-five (45) days prior written notice to Lessor. Lessee shall not, in this sole event, be obligated to or make any payments beyond the end of such fiscal period. Lessee agrees to surrender possession of the Equipment to the Lessor or its assignee on the date of such termination, prepared for shipment in accordance with manufacturer specifications and freight prepaid and insured to any location in the United States designated by Lessor. Lessor shall have all the rights and remedies to take possession of the Equipment and to sell, lease, or otherwise dispose of the Equipment as its own property without liability to Lessee.

Nonsubstitution

Since the inclusion of nonappropriation language grants college and university lessees an unconditional right to avoid future lease payment obligations in the event insufficient funds are appropriated, a nonsubstitution provision is frequently inserted in the lease to reduce the likelihood of abuse. The nonsubstitution clause precludes the college or university lessee from acquiring the same or similar equipment, facilities, or services for some length of time after an event of nonappropriation. It reduces the inherent risk of early termination of the lease for any reason other than insufficient appropriated funds. The nonsubstitution language might read as follows:

> If the provisions of the previous paragraph are utilized by Lessee, Lessee agrees not to purchase, lease, or rent equipment performing functions similar to those performed by the Equipment, and agrees not to permit functions similar to those performed through the use of the Equipment to be performed by its own employees or by any agency or entity affiliated with or hired by Lessee for the current period.

Essential Use

The essentiality of the facility or equipment is the key to avoidance of an event of nonappropriation by the college or university lessee. The more important or necessary a leased property is to the lessee, the less likely is an event of nonappropriation. Generally, lessors require that the college or university lessee provide a letter setting forth the essential nature of the leased property.

Nonappropriation language provides the legal basis for declaring that, for the purposes of state debt ceilings, a particular financial obligation is not debt. The essential use provision, coupled with the nonsubstitution clause, however, reassures the lessor that the lease will be honored, barring fiscal catastrophe.

Security Interest

As in the case of a commercial finance lease or conditional sale transaction, the college or university lessee usually grants a first security interest in the personal or real property to the lessor. Lessors frequently transfer title to the college or university lessee at the outset of the tax-exempt lease to avoid state or local property or ad valorem taxes. If a security interest to the lessor or his assigns is not granted, the lessor is considered an unsecured creditor.

Rating Criteria

In response to the growing use of lease transactions by all tax-exempt issuers, Standard & Poor's Corporation now rates tax-exempt lease transactions. Although all leases are not rated, larger or complicated transactions or those that will be sold publicly are frequently rated. These ratings on lease transactions are based on the credit-worthiness of the lessee, the essentiality of the leased property, and the security features and provisions of the lease.

Standard & Poor's requires the following documentation:
- A completed rating application
- A bond resolution or trust agreement
- An official statement or private placement memorandum
- The lease agreements
- An assignment agreement
- The lease payment schedule with principal and interest components and all concluding payment options
- A description of the lessee, its functions, services, management, and budgeting process
- A general description of the leased property

- A certificate of essential use, describing the purpose and function of the leased property, focusing on its importance in the performance of the lessee's services
- If applicable, a delivery and installation schedule, and a copy of the acceptable certificate if the property has already been delivered and accepted
- Bond counsel opinion.

Securities Law Considerations

Aside from debt limitation and federal income tax parameters of the tax-exempt lease, it is also necessary to consider the constraints imposed by securities law on this type of financing transaction.

The issue is whether the placing of a tax-exempt lease in the hands of an investor constitutes the sale of a security under the Securities Act of 1933. The Act prohibits the use of interstate commerce or the mails to sell a security unless there is either a registration statement in effect or some exemption from the Act itself.

If the assumption is made that the tax-exempt lease constitutes a security, two key exemptions are often employed to avoid formal registration. The exemptions are set forth in Sections 3a(2) and 4(2) of the Securities Act of 1933, as amended. The first, 3a(2), exempts governmental securities; the second, 4(2), exempts privately placed transactions.

To date, there has been no formal determination by the Securities and Exchange Commission that tax-exempt leases are securities within the meaning of the 1933 Act. However, in a letter to the Office of the Comptroller of the Currency, dated September 1, 1981, an SEC attorney held that tax-exempt lease participation interests are municipal obligations as that term is defined in Section 3(a)(29) of the Securities Exchange Act of 1934. This means that whenever a tax-exempt lease is assigned by a lessor to more than one institutional or retail investor, the offeror of those participation interests must conform with the applicable provisions of federal securities laws as interpreted by the Securities and Exchange Commission.

How Tax-Exempt Municipal Lease Financing Works

There are at least two parties in a tax-exempt lease: the lessor and the college or university lessee. In most transactions there is also an assignee of the lessor, which can be either an institutional or a retail investor.

The issuer can be a third-party lease broker, a commercial bank, a manufacturer, or an investment banker. In each instance, the lessor enters into the tax-exempt lease with a college or university that qualifies under Section 103 of the Internal Revenue Code.

Manufacturers and commercial banks who serve as lessors may retain the tax-exempt lease for their own portfolio or, like most lease brokers and investment bankers, may place the transaction with an institutional or retail investor. There are at least two forms that the assignment by the lessor to the investor can take. First, there may be a direct assignment of all the rights and none of the obligations, with payments by the college or university going directly to the investor. Second, there may be the same assignment to the investor in conjunction with the employment of a transfer agent. If the services of the transfer agent are utilized, its responsibilities include invoicing the college or university, receiving payments, forwarding the payments to the investor, and other administrative tasks.

When a transaction closes, the investor receives a legal opinion regarding the tax-exempt nature of the interest payments. In addition, there are several ancillary documents that vary with the particular type of transaction. A brief list of these documents includes:
- A legal opinion from the lessee's counsel regarding the legal, valid, and binding nature of the lease
- A certificate from the college or university lessee regarding the initial availability of funds
- An incumbency certificate
- A certificate of essential use
- A statement that the equipment being acquired is insured against loss
- A security interest instrument granting the lessor a first security interest in the property.

Benefits of the Tax-Exempt Lease

The tax-exempt lease affords the college or university lessee all the benefits of public facility or equipment ownership, the accrual of equity, and greater flexibility than traditional municipal bond financing methods. In addition, the typical tax-exempt lease provides for 100 percent financing and a full flow-through of warranties and guaranties. It may also be the least expensive or least desirable method of facility or equipment acquisition when compared with the issuance costs associated with municipal bond financing or the lack of ownership in an operating lease. When compared with the cash purchase option, the tax-exempt lease should be evaluated using a standard present-value discount-factor analysis.

Benefits of the Tax-Exempt Lease for Investors and Lessors

The obvious benefit of tax-exempt lease financing for investors is the tax-exempt interest component of the periodic payments by the college or university lessee. In addition, tax-exempt leases tend to be of a short or intermediate term, thus giving the investor or lessor a hedge against swings in an economic cycle. Further, tax-exempt leases often carry a higher interest rate than other tax-exempt obligations of comparable term. This interest rate differential may be the result of the absence of a rating by either Moody's or Standard & Poor's Corporation or the perceived risk associated with nonappropriation language.

Other advantages of the tax-exempt lease include the more frequent payment schedule and the regular repayment of principal and interest; this is unlike a municipal bond where the investor receives interest only until the maturity date of the bond. Monthly payment schedules are common, whereas municipal bonds pay interest semiannually. The more frequent payment schedule, the relatively short term, and the payback of principal and interest offer the investor an accelerated cash flow and an early return of invested capital.

Trends Influencing the Marketplace

Several trends characterize the evolving tax-exempt lease marketplace. They include an increase in dollar amount per lease, growing popularity among investors and lessees, broader applicability to real and personal property, and changing lease documentation.

The market for tax-exempt leases is divided into at least three dollar-volume categories: those leases for under $100,000, leases between $100,000 and $1 million, and the $1 million-plus category. The greatest annual dollar volume now occurs in the third category. One reason for this trend is the acceptance by institutional and retail customers of the low risk of nonappropriation by tax-exempt lessees. As the perception of risk declined during the last ten years, the yield to investors declined in direct proportion to the tax-exempt yields of comparable term general obligation bonds. College and university lessees, as a result, now pay a lower net interest cost for borrowed funds. In many instances tax-exempt leases are less expensive in terms of total borrowing costs than the more traditional general obligation bond. Because of the perception of risk associated with nonappropriation ten years ago, investors received premiums of 1 to 1.5 percent. Now tax-exempt leases are routinely priced at interest rates 0.25 to 0.5 percent over a comparable general obligation bond maturity.

Given its acceptance by institutional and retail investors and the lower interest rates paid by issuers, tax-exempt leases are used by a wide variety of qualified lessees to finance a wide range of real and personal property. Of the sixty-five tax-exempt leases rated by Standard & Poor's in 1985, forty-six covered real estate projects such as correctional facilities, utility projects, and parking facilities. Colleges and universities have used them for telephone systems, research equipment, computer, vehicles, administration, and campus buildings.

Tax-exempt lease documentation includes a variety of structuring techniques. Today it is common to see tax-exempt leases pooled with certificates of participation in the pool issued to investors. This approach allows smaller lessees to obtain lower interest rates by spreading the risk over a variety of lessees at sufficient dollar volumes to distribute certificates of participation to retail investors.

With the overall growth of tax-exempt leasing and its corresponding acceptance by lessees and investors, the tax-exempt lease marketplace now resembles more traditional public finance mechanisms. Although there is still no strong secondary market for tax-exempt leases, they can be adapted or enhanced to meet almost all needs expressed by manufacturers, colleges and universities, and investors. Tax-exempt leases can be rated, insured, or issued as certificates of participation. They can be made payable monthly, quarterly, semiannually, or annually. Tax-exempt leases have also been advance funded and structured to include reserve funds.

The Master Lease

The changing tax-exempt lease format also includes the master lease. The master lease structure differs from the conventional tax-exempt lease by providing a base document that has the capability of entering into present as well as future acquisitions of real or personal property. The document is structured with additional provisions to address future pricing, varying the lease term, and means of accounting for additional acquisitions. Once the terms of the base document are accepted, no new negotiation is required, and the process of acquisition is merely a procedural matter. A master tax-exempt lease allows the college or university to anticipate financial needs for several fiscal periods with the certainty of a known interest rate or a rate fixed to a published index. This structure is especially popular given the recent decline in interest rates. These lower interest rates have provided colleges and universities with the ability to refund outstanding obligations simultaneously with the issuance of new certificates of participation. By using the master lease, a college or university has funds available on a certain date. When equipment is delivered or construction completed, the lessee merely adds a payment schedule and equipment list to the master lease document.

Participation Certificate Market Increases

Investment banking firms dominate the certificate of participation market. Certificates of participation constitute securities and can only be offered to the retail marketplace by a broker/dealer registered with the National Association of Securities Dealers or the Securities and Exchange Commission. Certificates of participation differ from bonds in that they do not serve as evidence of public indebtedness nor do they carry the full faith and credit of the college or university. Yet the market for certificates has dramatically increased since they were first offered in 1978. Investors prefer the certificates' slightly greater yield and shorter average life span when compared with general obligation bonds. Investors have also discounted the risk of nonappropriation events because of their rarity.

Tax Reform Act of 1986

Despite uncertainty associated with the passage of new tax legislation by the U.S. House of Representatives on December 18, 1985, and nine months of subsequent deliberations by Senate and House conferees, the 1986 volume of tax-exempt leasing in the United States surged to almost $7.5 billion, a 50 percent increase over 1985. The Tax Reform Act of 1986 represents one of the most sweeping legislative reforms of the Internal Revenue Code since Section 103 was incorporated into the initial legislation in the early 1900s. The new law retains the substance of Section 103 (as reviewed in Clapp's chapter, this volume) but attempts to curtail future dollar volume and types of tax-exempt obligations. The rationale for enactment of this restrictive legislation stems from congressional concern that the U.S. Treasury is being deprived of monies through the issuance of a broad range of tax-exempt obligations.

The new tax legislation creates four categories of tax-exempt transactions: public purpose bonds, nongovernmental public purpose bonds, taxable municipal bonds, and certain bonds issued before August 7, 1986. Of the four categories, the group least affected by the Tax Reform Act are public purpose obligations, since they finance essential government functions. Tax-exempt leases fall into the public purpose category if they are used to finance the acquisition of essential personal property for use by qualifying issuers. The use test to determine whether obligations are public or nongovernmental purpose bonds will be met if 90 percent or more of the use is by a qualifying college or university and 90 percent or more of the payments are to be made by such users.

Although tax-exempt leases appear to be relatively unaffected by the 1986 act, interest rates paid by colleges or university lessees may increase due to new restrictions on the structuring of transactions, the disallowance of carrying charges to commercial banks, and the downward shift in individual tax brackets. Arbitrage earnings, once an integral part of structuring advanced funding and reserve clause provisions in tax-exempt leases, is severely restricted. Arbitrage earnings were derived by borrowing funds at tax-exempt rates and investing the proceeds in commercial accounts. Without those earnings, no offset in interest rates can be incorporated to reduce the borrowing costs to the issuer.

The Tax Reform Act of 1986 could also affect the overall pricing of tax-exempt leases by altering the mix of institutional and retail investors. Under the Act, banks will no longer be able to deduct the interest paid to carry tax-exempt obligations. Property and casualty insurance companies will be subject to a 15 percent charge on tax-exempt income for tax-exempt obligations acquired after August 7, 1986. With the drop in individual taxpayer brackets from a top of 50 percent to an effective 33 percent, the tax-exempt yield may have to increase to make these investments attractive to high-income individual taxpayers. Offsetting the above considerations are the disallowance of investment tax credit, the change in depreciation schedules, and the absence of other tax shelters. The net result will be higher yields paid to investors and higher interest rates charged to college and university lessees until the marketplace can digest the full impact of the Tax Reform Act of 1986.

Despite the Act's passage, tax-exempt leasing will continue to grow in popularity among governmental issuers and investors. Reasons for the growing popularity among college and university lessees include declining interest rate spreads when leasing is compared with other types of tax-exempt obligations, marketplace acceptance based on the full payout history of leases, ease of issuance, and the availability of numerous structuring options once thought appropriate only for general obligation bonds. Thus, although the Tax Reform Act of 1986 will change the complexion of the tax-exempt market, tax-exempt leasing will continue to increase in volume.

C. Gregory H. Eden is president of Eden Hannon & Company, a financial services and investment banking firm headquartered in Alexandria, Virginia.

Because higher education is becoming more expensive every year, there is a great need for new methods of financing.

Financing Tuition: Are Prepayment Plans the Right Answer?

Loren Hart

A private college education is becoming increasingly less affordable. This chapter discusses current and future financing mechanisms that could help make a private college education more affordable. Special attention will be paid to today's most widely discussed financing mechanism—tuition prepayment plans, or tuition futures—mechanisms that allow families to save now in anticipation of rising college costs. The newly enacted Tax Reform Act of 1986, which eliminates some traditional ways to save for college, accentuates the need for such programs.

Tuition Mechanisms: Only a Partial Solution

It is easy to overestimate the importance of any financing mechanism in making any product, including a college education, more affordable. All the current publicity about tuition prepayment programs as the salvation of higher education requires that these programs be put into perspective. The affordability of any product depends on four basic factors.
- The base price of the product
- The amount of the consumer's income the product takes

- The willingness of the buyer to spend more (or less) income than before to buy the product (price elasticity/inelasticity)
- Financing mechanisms that make the base price more affordable (or at least seem more affordable).

Breaking down the elements of affordability helps show that if larger shares of family income are required to pay for college, either families must be willing to devote a larger share of their income to pay for college or financing mechanisms must be developed to make it easier for them to pay.

Private Colleges Increasingly Less Affordable. The data is disturbing. Recent research, reported by Terry Hartle (1986) in the *Educational Record*, points out that between academic years 1980-81 and 1985-86, prices at private universities and private four-year colleges increased 69 percent and 62 percent respectively. During this period, the median income for all families increased only 29 percent, the median income for families with dependents aged eighteen to nineteen in college increased by only 40 percent, and the Consumer Price Index rose 31 percent. The deterioration in affordability is even more serious for selective private institutions. Hartle reports that higher education prices as a percentage of median family income for families with dependents aged eighteen to nineteen in college have increased from 24 to 29 percent during the period 1980-86 for private universities in general. However, the increase was from 35 to 42 percent for Hartle's sample of selective private institutions. On a more positive note, Hartle's data shows a significantly less serious deterioration in the ability to pay for public sector higher education.

Private college administrators are well aware that their product is becoming less affordable. The basic responses so far have been to (1) justify the price increases, (2) rely on the buyer's continued willingness to pay (price elasticity), and (3) find workable financing mechanisms.

The justifiers point to a number of reasons why private college costs are so high.
1. Colleges did not pass along to students many of the inflationary results of the 1970s. Faculty and staff salaries, over 50 percent of the budget in most private colleges, must catch up significantly. Other problems deferred from the 1970s include maintenance and updating of equipment and research facilities.
2. Costs for libraries, computers, scientific equipment, and especially for internally financed student aid continue to rise faster than inflation.
3. There are continuing management problems because of a relatively inflexible labor pool of entrenched tenured faculty.

Ultimately, of course, justifications are useless because the consumer neither knows nor cares about the provider's costs or production problems. If the price gets too high, the consumer will not buy the product.

Consumers will not buy a product unless, of course, the consumer is price inelastic. Behind much of the thinking for the substantially above-inflation price increases in private college tuition is the assumption that virtually no matter what the price of a private college education is relative to a family's income, the family will pay because private education is so important. This is a very dangerous assumption. No matter what past data show about the price inelasticity of the cost of a private college education, prices are now at very high levels, and past relationships need not necessarily be repeated in the future.

Fears that price inelasticity may be over have prompted some colleges to move, however slowly, toward financing mechanisms. However, I feel strongly that financing plans can only do so much to make a product more affordable, and the private college industry should not rely on financing mechanisms too heavily but instead continue to work on product price control.

Here are two brief examples: In the 1970s housing shot up in value and housing prices increased faster than family income. The housing industry did benefit from some price inelasticity (buyers were willing to put more of their income into housing). But the industry also modified and tried to control the price of the product (smaller houses, townhouses, condominiums) and developed new financing mechanisms (variable rate mortgages, seller financing) to make housing more affordable. The health care industry is a less happy example. Health care costs increased dramatically over inflation in the 1970s and early 1980s. The industry had to be substantially restructured by the government and employers, who then shouldered the increased costs. The health care industry relied too much on the buyer's continued willingness to accept larger and larger price increases.

Tuition Savings Plans Not a Substitute. Tuition savings plans and similar mechanisms probably will be used primarily by upper-middle-class and upper-class families who can save money for a college education. Lower-income families understandably have difficulty saving money.

Financial aid will continue to help make private colleges more affordable for the majority, but maintaining financial aid programs will be difficult. There is increasing pressure on college budgets to limit grant aid. Family loan programs are proliferating, but there is concern about how much debt a student can realistically handle. Most nonguaranteed loan programs have credit requirements that may be too strict for lower- and middle-class families. The pressure on financial aid is being caused by decreases in real dollars in federal support as well as price increases. For example, a recent Joint Economic Committee of Congress Report (Hansen, 1987) showed that in constant 1986 dollars, total federal financial aid had fallen from $18.4 billion in 1980-81 to $15.7 billion estimated for 1985-86—a 14.7 percent decrease.

The Tax Reform Act of 1986 does not help this situation. Interest on student loans is no longer deductible unless those loans are incorporated into a second mortgage. This will raise the cost of borrowing for students and their families. Taxation of scholarships and fellowships for other than tuition and equipment will also hurt. Obviously, the concern here is that financial aid (especially internally generated grant aid) will have to be increased.

Many private colleges are indirectly funding more scholarships through tuition increases. As private college prices increase faster than family income, more students become eligible for financial aid and eligible students get more financial aid. Although the percentage of students receiving aid must increase, private colleges will still rely on significant percentages of the student body (over 50 percent in many cases) who do not receive financial aid. This means that there is still a net benefit for a college to raise its prices substantially higher than family income and simultaneously to maintain a "needs blind" admissions policy. A 10 percent price increase may produce only a 6.5 percent increase in revenue after increased scholarship aid is deducted, but this is still a 6.5 percent gain. Of course, what is happening is that well-to-do parents are paying for part of the increased financial aid for poorer students. Parents with a high enough income, whose children are ineligible for aid, are asked to contribute a higher percentage of their income for private college costs. There are obvious dangers in carrying out this policy too long. As prices continue to increase faster than family income, the net return from tuition increases (net after increased scholarship aid is subtracted) should keep declining and higher-income parents may rebel against the "Robin Hood" effect.

Proposed Tuition Programs May Not Meet Needs of Students or Colleges. Tuition savings plans must meet the needs of large numbers of parents (so that they will save through the plans) as well as the needs of a large number of private colleges (who would participate in the plan). But the currently proposed single college plans and state-sponsored plans do not provide enough choice to meet the needs of large numbers of families or colleges.

Any tuition savings plan must meet the needs of substantial numbers of families. Private college costs are increasing faster than families' ability to pay, and at the same time the standard means of saving for college are inadequate. Income generated from traditional savings plans (such as investments in stocks and bonds) is taxed. Under the new tax law, capital gains no longer receive special treatment, so there is less of an advantage to cashing in on stocks to pay for education. One traditional tax shelter, saving in a child's name through the Uniform Gifts to Minors Act, is now subject to tax disadvantages (income over $1,000 is taxed at the parents' tax rates).

Single College Plans Too Risky. Although parents want a savings plan for college, they do not want to sacrifice choice in determining the kind of education they and their children want. A college education is not a commodity like salt, which can be purchased without concern for the brand. There is much risk to parents in joining a single college plan: Will the child want to go to college at all? Will the child be admitted to the preselected college? Will the child want to go to the preselected college even if admitted? Will the preselected college be of sufficient quality and have the appropriate programs in the future to make the college acceptable to parents and student? Over time, colleges may increase in quality (and become more selective, so that a child may not necessarily be admitted) or decrease in quality (so that a child would not want to go). Highly selective colleges could not establish single college programs because there would be either too great a risk that the student would not be admitted or too much pressure on the admissions office to admit the student.

Single college plans have a very limited market and will have very limited impact on the affordability of private higher education. But they could be used by traditionally less selective colleges to help stabilize their enrollment.

Lack of choice is a fundamental concern about single college plans such as the pioneer effort at Duquesne University that has offered parents the opportunity to prepurchase tuition for their young children. In the Duquesne and similar plans, the parent deposits a relatively small amount of money ($4,000-$8,000) in return for four years of guaranteed tuition when the child reaches college age. Plans that follow the Duquesne model have limited withdrawal provisions if the child does not attend the particular college. To make up for these restrictions, most plans sell at a significant discount to current tuition. For example, the University of Detroit quoted what they expect will be a $91,841 four-year tuition cost in 2004 at $6,412 in 1986; this assumes over 14 percent per annum in compound interest at a time when twenty-year Treasury bonds were earning 8 percent. Obviously, colleges selling tuition at a large discount expect significant numbers of students never to use the program, and they can profit if they are right (and lose if they are wrong). Colleges can encourage participants who do not use the prepaid tuition to donate unused tuition programs to the colleges so at least the participant gets a tax deduction.

Insufficient Choice in State-Sponsored Programs. The proposals for state-sponsored programs are clearly a step in the right direction. But not even state-sponsored programs can offer broad enough choices to be sufficiently attractive to large numbers of families who may be interested in private colleges. The pioneer Michigan proposal, for example, covers only public institutions. The proposed New Jersey and Massachusetts plans for state-sponsored college programs would allow private colleges as well as public universities to participate.

These three state plans are limited to in-state residents. Since Americans move around quite a bit, state programs could guarantee in-state tuition even if the family moves out of state, provided the family members were residents when they entered the program. It is not clear if this proposal would increase the number of in-state tuition students at public institutions. But even this solution may not offer enough choice. A New Jersey family, for example, that moves to Texas might find it better to send their child to the University of Texas than to an equally good New Jersey state university. Thus, even families interested primarily in public higher education may be concerned that a state plan is too limiting.

Parents who are seriously interested in private higher education will find state-sponsored plans very limiting. The proposed New Jersey and Massachusetts plans allow only private colleges in the state to participate. The majority of students in many private colleges are from out of state. What happens to the New Jersey family that wants to consider private colleges in Maine, Minnesota, and Oregon? Therefore, state plans that include only in-state private colleges may not be that attractive. Also if a state limits the amount of tuition a private college can receive, it is doubtful that many private colleges will be interested in participating.

Governors and state legislators can derive a lot of political mileage from state-sponsored tuition savings programs that try to make higher education more affordable. But other than political mileage, there does not seem to be a strong rationale for limiting programs to the state. Higher education is a national market.

A National Program Would Offer the Most Choice. The best tuition savings program would cover a large number of schools nationwide. A successful program must meet the needs of participating colleges, and the most basic need is that the program not limit their ability to determine their own tuition. Therefore, to be acceptable to a number of private colleges, the program should not guarantee the actual tuition at the school (or not guarantee tuition except to the extent that a participating college agrees). This could be accommodated through an index system: Tuition at a participating institution could be calculated each year as a percentage of a standard tuition unit. A standard tuition unit might buy 2.1 college credits at a community college and 0.34 credits at an expensive private college. This index program could accommodate a wide variety of schools and programs (from community colleges to private medical schools) and other pricing variations (part-time attendance, summer session, and so on). A family could purchase the amount of tuition units it needs and can afford consistent with the type of institutions in which it is interested. Data could be kept showing historical relationships between the index price of the standard tuition unit and the tuition unit cost of the institution or group of institutions of interest to the family.

Tax Advantages Must Be Built into the System

Much attention has been justifiably given to the tax advantages of these plans. To be attractive, the interest return from the original payments in these plans must compound tax free to allow for maximum growth. These programs will not be attractive to parents if the interest return is taxed each year.

A tuition savings plan could be tax exempt for one of three reasons: (1) Congress legislates that such plans are tax exempt, (2) the structure of a plan renders it tax exempt, or (3) the plan invests only in tax-exempt investments.

Congressional Acts and Tax Exemption. Legislation as a way of making college savings plans tax exempt should not be ignored. Congress has declared investments in qualified pension funds to be tax exempt. Congress may see that higher education is so important to the nation's future that saving for college should be tax exempt. There have even been proposals for "educational" IRAs. I think a national IRA is the best tuition savings plan possible; however, this must be considered a long-term solution in light of the current post-tax reform legislative environment.

The Search for Tax-Exempt Structures. Of the remaining two alternatives, it is better that the plan itself rather than the investments in the plan be structured as tax exempt. If the plan itself is tax exempt, its investments can be placed in higher yielding taxable investments of stocks and bonds without tax liability. Yet the potential for a tortuous plan structure in an attempt to make the plan tax exempt could result in a loss of flexibility and choice.

A basic way to make the structure tax exempt is to make what in many respects is a savings and investment plan *not be* a savings and investment plan. The plan can be structured so that the family is buying tuition now to be used in the future—a tuition contract. For instance, if I bought a bottle of red wine fifteen years ago for $4, stored it, and now drink it, I do not pay capital gains even though that bottle of wine is now worth $54. If I buy a contract to take delivery of 100 bushels of wheat at $2 per bushel, and one year from now I take delivery when it is $3 per bushel, I will not pay taxes on the implicit $1 per bushel gain. However, if I am a speculator in the futures market and sell the future contract rather than take delivery, I do pay taxes on the grain gain.

The bottle of wine analogy works well for single college plans like Duquesne's. This is especially true because withdrawal is either not allowed or allowed with only the original payment refunded (and therefore no taxable gain). Duquesne and institutions with similar plans have applied to the IRS for a ruling on their plans. But the bottle of wine analogy works less well for a plan that involves many colleges, especially ones that allow withdrawal for cash gain.

Withdrawal as a Key Tax Issue. The withdrawal feature is most important from a tax standpoint. The more liberal the withdrawal terms, the more tax problems the plan has. It seems clear that the most attractive withdrawal plan would be taxable. If participants may withdraw the full value of the plan in cash (the original price plus accumulated interest), the accumulated interest would be subject to income tax at ordinary income tax rates now that the Tax Reform Act has eliminated capital gains. In other words, if a family buys a tuition contract for $1,000 and cashes it in for $2,200 ten years later because the child does not want to go to college, the family would pay regular income tax on the $1,200 gain. Some tax experts worry that the right to withdraw cash might subject all participating families to (1) an annual tax on the implicit interest earned through the plan even though interest was not actually received or (2) a tax on implicit gain under the tuition contract, which is known as the constructive receipt doctrine (one could have had the cash but did not take it). This is comparable to having the implied interest on zero coupon bonds taxed each year, even though the investor does not receive the interest, or the implied gain on taxable stock distributions taxed, even though the stock has not yet sold.

A version of the Michigan plan explicitly recognized this problem by offering a choice of two plans. In Plan A only the nominal purchase price can be withdrawn. In Plan B a participant may withdraw the purchase price plus accumulated interest. Many tax experts worry that the right to withdraw in Plan B could create a tax liability for all participants in Plan B, not just those who actually do withdraw, because under the constructive receipt doctrine, cash earnings were *available* to all.

Flexible Tax-Exempt Withdrawal Plans Might Be Developed

The tax environment is very uncertain, but people are scurrying to develop plans free from tax but still sufficiently attractive to parents. The current thrust is to devise a plan where cash withdrawals are not allowed or are severely penalized but offer the contract purchaser sufficient flexibility so that the purchaser will be unlikely to withdraw. Of course, tax lawyers worry that the more flexibility there is, the more the program will seem like an investment and be subject to taxes. Elements of potential flexibility include:

1. *Secondary market withdrawal only.* The plan sponsor promises no residual interest (no right to withdraw from the plan) but will create a secondary market with the contract units (so that a student attending a participating college could buy through the secondary market slightly discounted tuition from the family who will not use the contract units).

Because the plan itself does not set a residual value, there is a strong argument that those participants who do not withdraw should not pay taxes. Participants who sell the units would probably still be subject to income tax on the gains. This approach seems far better than a plan like Michigan's Plan B, which could subject all participants to tax liability.

2. *Broad college participation.* In the most ideal plan, contract units could be used at almost any college in the nation. There is no hard-and-fast rule here, but most tax lawyers worry that a contract that could be used anywhere looks too much like an investment. No one knows the magic limit on participating colleges, but more than fifty causes concern from a tax standpoint.

3. *Limited transferability of benefits.* While no transferability of benefits is the safest from a tax standpoint, it is probably safe to provide some limited right of transfer. This limited right could be extended to all other siblings in the family, or it might allow the purchaser to designate a small number of specific beneficiaries. If the benefit can be transferred without restriction, there are likely to be tax consequences.

4. *Flexible timing of use of prepurchased tuition.* The contract units should be structured so that the participants can use their tuition credits at any time. There should be no specific tax problem with this, but caution is advisable. As tuition levels rise, so do the fund's investments; flexible timing in use should not create an insurmountable problem for the plan sponsor. Of course, if tuition is sold at a discount, a minimum time lapse or "first year of use" may be required.

Other Areas of Flexibility. A number of items that add to the flexibility of plans may not, in and of themselves, have important tax consequences. These include:

1. *Unlimited participation (any individual or family can participate).* State plans need not be limited to in-state residents. Of course, the price to out-of-state residents would be based on out-of-state rates. Unlimited participation is especially helpful to private college participants, which rely heavily on students from other states. Although unlimited participation may not in itself hurt the tax-exempt status, it might weigh heavily when combined with other unfavorable elements.

2. *Abilities to borrow the purchase price (extended payment).* This could make the plan especially attractive. A family could provide now for future tuition with low monthly payments. The fact that nonmortgage interest is no longer deductible under the Tax Reform Act can be a negative factor, but perhaps deductible second-mortgage loan plans could be devised for this purpose. At the very least, some form of extended payment plan could be devised as opposed to one lump-sum payment.

3. *Minimized purchase price.* There is no need to require a family to purchase four years of full undergraduate tuition. Tuition units in small denominations could be sold, but not so small as to be administratively

costly. The mutual fund industry, for example, uses $1,000 to $3,000 initial purchase minimums and $250 to $500 subsequent purchase minimums, which are small enough to attract interest but not so small as to be administratively costly.

Tax Status of the Plan. The issue, therefore, is whether a sufficiently flexible plan can be constructed that meets family needs but is also tax exempt (and can be invested in higher yielding taxable investments). This issue will probably not be resolved soon. The question is one of degree. How much flexibility can be added before the plan seems like an investment vehicle and not a present purchase of a product to be used in the future (like the bottle of wine). Each element of flexibility may be fine in its own right, but together could make the plan a taxable investment vehicle. The first plan to be submitted to the IRS will have important ramifications for those that follow.

Perhaps too many sacrifices will have to be made to make the plan structure tax exempt. The most unacceptable areas of sacrifice would be:
- Limiting the number of colleges to a small group (less than fifty) or the geographic location to a single state (although state location should not make a difference for tax purposes)
- Limiting the number of families that could participate in the plan
- Forcing the participating colleges to guarantee the tuition rate.

A Plan with Tax-Exempt Investments. There is a simple way to ensure that the plan is not taxable to individual participants under current tax law: The plan should only invest in tax-exempt investments, making it essentially a savings plan. The two most obvious tax-exempt investment vehicles for such a plan would be tax-exempt municipal bonds and single-premium life insurance policies. Currently, single-premium life insurance policies carry a higher return (and offer greater flexibility for the plan sponsor). It is important to note, however, that plans such as these may have to be pure savings plans, not tuition guarantee plans. The tuition guarantee itself could be separate taxable investment from the underlying investments that fund the plan. It may still be possible to have a tuition guarantee program if, for example, an insurance company guarantees that the return on single premium life insurance policies will keep up with a standard tuition unit. As yet no company has offered to take this risk.

A tuition savings plan with solid tax-exempt returns, national participation for almost any college, available to all families, and having the right to withdraw without tax effects (a key feature of savings plans funded with tax-exempt investments) may be preferable to a significantly more restrictive plan (fewer college participants, taxable gains on withdrawals) that offers a somewhat higher return because it invests in taxable investments. Participating colleges and universities could become marketers for a national tuition savings plan that could have a respectable return because of limited marketing and administrative costs. The savings plan that was invested in tax-exempt instruments could have all the beneficial features described above and any other elements thought desirable. These might include:

1. Withdrawal of funds without tax effect. The full value (original investment plus income) would always be available to the investor. In a true savings plan there would be no need to restrict withdrawal, unless a form of tuition guarantee was involved.

2. No limit to the number of families permitted to participate.

3. No limit to the number of colleges and universities (public and private) allowed to participate.

4. Ability to save in small amounts (as small as administratively feasible). Extended payment should be possible.

5. Ability to borrow up to 100 percent of the amount purchased. There would be no credit concerns, since the amount invested would serve as collateral for the amount borrowed. If connected with a second mortgage, the loan could be tax deductible (with the possible exception of loans invested in tax-exempt bonds). The loan could perhaps be funded with a low-cost student loan program. Careful calculations would have to be made in each case to see if it made sense for the parent to borrow to make the payments.

6. Unlimited transferability of benefits (because withdrawal would not be taxable).

7. Completely flexible timing in the use of the tuition.

Marketing Through Colleges. Any program should be marketed through participating colleges rather than through private firms like insurance companies or brokerage houses. Not only should this hold down marketing costs, but it would demonstrate to the public that colleges are doing something to make education more affordable.

Financial Risk of Participating Institutions

It is unlikely that many colleges and universities would be interested in guaranteeing their tuition to any significant degree. Colleges will want to control how much tuition would be subject each year to guarantees. This points to an indexed system where standard tuition units (the index) are exchanged for tuition at various percentages. An index system is a savings system, not a guarantee to meet tuition at a particular college. The number of units the purchaser originally buys to fund four years of highly priced private college tuition, for example, may not be sufficient if the standard index unit or the return on an uninsured fund does not increase as fast as the expensive private tuition.

If the mechanism is purely a savings plan with no guarantee of meeting increases in the standard tuition unit (or an individual college's tuition), there is no financial risk to the plan sponsor. The family that participates takes the risk that the savings return will not keep pace with tuition increases.

If there is to be a guarantee of meeting tuition costs, there is the risk that the investment returns might not meet the tuition increases. This risk could be assumed either by the participating colleges (individually or collectively), a public agency (the state itself or a state agency), a nonprofit corporation formed for the purpose, or a for-profit corporation. Although an individual college could assume the risk for its own tuition costs, it might be difficult to persuade colleges to assume the risk for another college's tuition costs. A state legislature can control prices of public colleges in the state, so it could assume the risk for a state plan where the standard tuition unit is pegged to the state university tuition. Otherwise, noncollege entities (states, nonprofit, and for-profit corporations) are likely to worry about price increases they cannot control, and therefore they might want to share the risk with participating colleges. The complications in negotiating shares of the financial risk could make a pure savings plan easier to establish on a broad scale.

Summary

Financing mechanisms are needed to help make a college education, especially a private college education, more affordable. Financing mechanisms alone will not solve the affordability problem: Cost controls in the private colleges are the most effective solution.

Tuition savings plans could be an excellent financing mechanism to help make college tuition more affordable. The current plans offered by individual colleges and the proposed state plans, however, offer families too limited a choice. These plans ignore the fact that a college education is a highly specialized product, not a commodity. A broad plan covering as many colleges as possible (which could be an unlimited number in a pure savings plan) and an unlimited number of participating families (without regard for their states of residence) should attract the most interest and do the most good.

Crucial to the success of these plans will be whether or not participating families are exempt from taxes on the interest earned on their payments. Most of the effort so far has been to look for ways to make these plans other than savings plans for IRS purposes. However, too much choice and flexibility may have to be sacrificed in making these plans tax exempt. An alternative is to consider a savings plan that only invests in tax exempt investments (such as single-premium life insurance policies). The flexibility and choices offered could outweigh the fact that such savings plans offer a lower yield and do not guarantee that the return will keep pace with tuition increases.

References

Hansen, J. S. "Student Loans: Are They Overburdening a Generation?" *Chronicle of Higher Education,* 1987, *33* (17), 18-22.
Hartle, T. W. "Beneath the Surface: College Is Not as Costly as It Seems." *Educational Record,* 1986, *67* (2-3), 16-19.

Loren Hart is vice-president and treasurer of Swarthmore College.

Managing and exploiting intellectual property is a great challenge for the contemporary university administrator.

Equity Financing: Research Partnerships

Michael B. Goldstein

When presidents, trustees, and others responsible for our nation's colleges and universities search for alternatives for financing the costs of building, equipping, and running their institutions, they almost uniformly look to approaches that exploit their school's tangible assets, most often the real property. Indeed, the creative use of institutional land holdings represents a great opportunity for a college to convert underutilized assets into financially productive ones.

However, there is another category of asset unique to colleges and universities that represents an even more significant opportunity for enhancing the present and future economic position of an institution. That asset is the knowledge created within the institution in the course of research carried out by its faculty, students, and other personnel. The effective and appropriate exploitation of this asset—the intellectual property of a college or university—represents one of the current challenges for higher education.

Academia and the Sale of Knowledge

Any discussion of the exploitation of institutionally created property must begin with a set of caveats dealing as much with what is appropriate as with what is effective. First, one must acknowledge the unique environment and ethos of academia: The generation of knowledge is not usually considered a product in the same way that private industry regards the inventions of its scientists and engineers.

Some will argue that it is an essential purpose of higher education, unlike its profit-driven counterparts, to give the knowledge it develops to the world without regard for economic gain. They argue that what distinguishes universities from businesses is the freedom for their faculties to pursue knowledge for its own sake. To pursue profits, these observers continue, is to pervert the academic enterprise, diminish academic freedom, and ultimately reduce the very scope and quality of the knowledge being created.

These academic traditionalists conclude that when the economic value of knowledge becomes important to the institution, the process of knowledge creation is skewed in an inappropriate fashion. In their view, the pursuit of knowledge becomes subordinate to the pursuit of revenues and destroys the special place of higher education as a sanctuary removed from such pressures.

These arguments should not be dismissed or treated lightly. First, it is true that colleges and universities are not like other enterprises. Their fundamental purposes are different, a distinction recognized by society in granting such institutions relief from so fundamental an obligation as the payment of income taxes. One reason for this benefit is the expectation that the knowledge created will be made available for the benefit of society. And, unlike most businesses, colleges and universities are uniquely collegial entities, with power shared across several parallel hierarchies, diffuse decision-making processes, and a venerable history of independence among the faculty. To speak of exploiting that knowledge for economic gain, even if exploitation supports the bona fide pursuits of that institution, runs against the grain of many who wield significant institutional authority. This resistance, if not overcome, can easily doom any effort to capitalize on the value of an institution's intellectual property. But the value of that asset, whether real or potential, is becoming so great and the need to use it so acute that the approaches of the past, to which many faculty have become accustomed and with which they are comfortable, are no longer adequate to the task at hand. The substance of this examination, then, is to identify ways through which an institution can exploit the knowledge created under its auspices, consistent with its unique status as an academic enterprise.

Licensing and Royalties: A Piece of the Pie

Colleges and universities have historically acted, if sometimes haltingly, to guarantee themselves a share in the value of the knowledge created by their researchers. This has commonly taken the form of the assertion of property rights (that is, the perfecting of patents and copyrights) in inventions and discoveries and the licensing of those rights for commercial exploitation. There are institutions, particularly those engaged in agricultural research, that have long received significant revenues from the licensing of discoveries made by their faculty members.

One problem with straight licensing is that the income derived is usually limited to a modest percentage of the net profit of the commercial product arising out of the discovery. Although royalties can provide a significant revenue stream over time, their near-term economic effects are usually limited. Further, because royalties follow only after the discovery has been successfully exploited, any income produced does little to support other research and even less to provide capital support. Finally, the licensee looks to its own interests in exploiting the licensed discovery, which may include holding the discovery off the market until a present product is fully exploited. Although a good licensing agreement can guard against such warehousing, it is astonishing how often institutions have allowed this to take place. Even when the licensing agreement gives the institution the right to recapture the discovery if it is not exploited within a specified period, the lapsed time may substantially reduce the discovery's value and its potential for relicensure.

This last problem has become particularly severe in several important areas where the volatility of the marketplace makes the rather leisurely process of patent protection obsolete: Second and third generations of a discovery, sufficiently different to avoid infringement, may appear long before patent protection can be perfected. In such cases, the key to successful exploitation is how quickly an idea can be rushed to market—a concept utterly foreign to the nature and organization of higher education.

Sponsored Research: Buying into the System

To afford institutions more benefit from their generation of knowledge and to respond to the accelerating needs of industry for access to the products of that knowledge, many schools have engaged since World War II in sponsored research. This research consists of several activities ranging from government research grants, in which the institution may retain substantial property rights in discoveries arising out of the work performed under the grants, to contract research, in which such rights are granted in advance and in their entirety to the sponsoring commercial entity. The advantage of the sponsored-research approach is its ability to generate current income for the conduct of research, including funds for the acquisition of costly research instrumentation. In recent years the tax laws have encouraged the contribution of research instrumentation by granting significant economic benefits to donors, who also may benefit from the fruits of research conducted on the equipment.

Yet sponsored research still fails to provide the institution with access to the true value of the knowledge created by its faculty. The degree to which that is the case may readily be measured by the steady flow of productive faculty from their academic posts to positions with commercial concerns, notably so-called start up companies. The inducement is not just better equipment, availability of more support staff, or even a higher salary. Rather, it is the opportunity to share in the value created by the discovery that lures many of the brightest and most productive researchers away from their campus laboratories. And well it should. A faculty member who moves to the profit sector will be given a substantial share in the equity (stock) of the company. Although the stock is initially worthless, 100,000 shares in a successful project could make the researcher a wealthy person. The loss of the real pleasures of teaching and academic collegiality—not to mention the rather more questionable "delights" of begging for equipment, facilities, and graduate assistants—can be overcome by the prospect of economic returns far beyond anything possible in higher education.

It is not only the faculty researcher who feels this tension. The institution finds itself looking at the conduct of research within its halls and the profits made by the sponsors of the research. Their support may indeed be generous, enabling the school to acquire costly equipment and hire needed support personnel, but it may also be a minuscule fraction of the true value of the discoveries. How to capture that value, consistent with the values and ethos of a higher education institution and the law is a key question for the modern college or university.

Research Partnerships: The New Frontier

One solution that is gaining considerable currency is the creation of research partnerships. Unlike licensing programs and sponsored research, research partnerships cast the institution in the role of part owner of the asset value of the fruits of research. This approach circumvents a major limitation of tax-exempt status: the inability to sell a share of equity to acquire the capital needed to support the development and commercial exploitation of research. In the simplest form, an institution enters into an agreement with a commercial concern to create a new legal entity, a partnership or a corporation in which the commercial partner and the institution together hold the entirety of the shares. Although the formed entity may be either a corporation or a partnership, the term *research partnership* will be used here to mean either one. Each partner may own an equal share of the equity of the research partnership, or one may have a majority interest. However, minority ownership does not necessarily imply loss of control, because the partnership agreement sets forth the rights of all parties under particular circumstances. The institution brings to the partnership the rights to certain present or potential discoveries of its researchers, and the commercial partner brings the financial and business resources needed to carry out the work. The partnership can also borrow money in its own name, creating another source of funds for capital equipment and facilities without increasing direct institutional debt. The rights arising from the research are assigned to the partnership, which may either directly seek their commercial exploitation or enter into a joint venture with the commercial partner to exploit them. If the research results in an exploitable discovery and that discovery proves an economic success, the value-added of the discovery enhances the asset value of the partnership, which in turn creates a valuable asset for the institution. The institution may satisfy itself with the revenue stream derived from the partnership's exploitation of the discovery, or it may sell all or a portion of its share in the partnership for whatever the market will bear.

This simple model is fine for illustrative purposes. But in reality it is far from the perfect design. It implies that the partnership will be carrying out the research, thus causing it to be removed from the auspices of the institution. That is just what many faculty fear most: the establishment of profit-oriented peripheral facilities that are not subject to the checks and balances of academia. Under certain circumstances, this outcome is not undesirable, but the research partnership approach allows for a different configuration that speaks quite directly to these faculty concerns.

One solution is to have the research partnership enter into a sponsored-research contract with the institution itself for the conduct of the desired research. The sponsored-research agreement would provide for the assignment of any discoveries to the partnership, which in turn would be responsible for their commercial exploitation. In return, the research partnership would pay the cost of carrying out the research in the same fashion as departmental research is currently supported through sponsored-research contracts. This places the responsibility for the actual conduct of the research within the academic institution in a form that is understandable by faculty, trustees, and other interested parties.

Using Research Partnerships

The research partnership can also provide the institution with access to the appropriate research instrumentation and facilities. Obviously, the partnership can simply give the institution the equipment and facilities as part of its consideration of the assignment of discoveries. But it can also acquire the equipment and facilities and make them available to the institution and its researchers for the specific purpose of carrying out the sponsored research. The research partnership uses its own which it then leases to the institution for the conduct of research, in exchange for the assignment of the rights to the discoveries. There may be significant economic advantages to this latter approach, particularly with the tightening of the Tax Code provisions relative to the determination of when equipment and facilities are deemed to be in the service of tax-exempt entities and therefore subject to less desirable depreciation and other tax treatment. At the end of the lease term (and assuming the proper steps have been taken to comport with the requirements of the Tax Code), the research partnership can donate the equipment and facilities to the institution, affording itself a further tax advantage and of course further benefiting the institution. Changes wrought under the 1986 Tax Reform Act prescribe rather more rigorous tests for such transactions, but they remain viable as long as properly executed.

Affording an institution the use of equipment and facilities instead of providing the funds for the institution to acquire or build facilities may also avoid other concerns that often plague institutional research endeavors, particularly those at public universities. Public institutions must follow a complex and often time-consuming procurement process to acquire equipment and build facilities, a process that can be avoided if the research partnership does the acquiring and building. Further, many states stringently limit the ability of their public institutions to allow the commercial use of their own facilities. Although sponsored research is generally an exception, if the research partnership develops other programs (or other uses of the equipment and facilities) apart from those covered by the sponsored-research agreement, state law might inhibit that use. Likewise, if a public or private institution uses equipment purchased by the partnership but installed in a building erected with tax-exempt funding, the use of that equipment might jeopardize the tax-exempt status of the building financing—a most undesirable outcome.

Another problem with the simple partnership model is the question of the ability and wisdom of the institution's being a partner in such an enterprise. There are several reasons why this might not be prudent. First, for some public universities, state laws may restrict the participation of such institutions in commercial activities. Second, income from the partnership may increase unrelated business taxable income (UBTI). Although UBTI is not, as some seem to think, a four-letter obscenity destined to result in the loss of institutional tax exemption (it is, after all a nonconfiscatory tax on net profits), it needs to be considered from a purely economic perspective.

There is also the question of liability. Liability arising from an institution's participation in a research partnership can take two basic forms. One form is responsibility for the debts and obligations arising from the operations of the research partnership. That responsibility is unlimited if the institution is a general (that is, participating in management) partner.

the institution is a general (that is, participating in management) partner. If the research partnership should fail, the institution must avoid responsibility for paying partnership debts with its general funds. Even more significant, however, is the risk of being held liable for unforeseen events. Particularly in such fields as the biological sciences where the risk of negligence lawsuits looms large, a responsible institution must do everything possible to insulate its academic enterprise from a costly lawsuit.

Finally, there is the question of control and of the ability and wisdom of higher education management to assume responsibility for the conduct of the research partnership. A common cause of failure of creative financing efforts by colleges and universities is the unwillingness of the administration to relinquish control of the general management of the institution. Running a college is a full-time job for the president and chief financial officer, and taking on responsibility for running another complex enterprise can overload the system. Most college presidents did not rise through the ranks of corporate America, and thus their training, experience, and attitudes are not necessarily those needed for managing a potentially very complex commercial enterprise.

Subsidiaries and Intermediaries: Protecting the Interests of the Academic Enterprise

A solution adopted by an increasing number of institutions is the creation of one or more intermediary entities, to stand between the institution and the research partnership. For public universities this is often a two-stage arrangement, with the university creating or using an existing nonprofit entity often called a university foundation. The foundation in turn is the sole shareholder in a for-profit holding corporation, which is the active partner in the research partnership. The holding corporation may provide overhead services to the research partnership, and, of considerable importance, it can serve the same function for any number of such entities. This structure serves several useful purposes.

1. It may limit the liability of the institution for the debts and obligations of the research partnership or incidents arising out of the acts or negligence of the partnership.

2. For the public university, it takes the ownership or an involvement in the research partnership out of the direct purview of the state education bureaucracy.

3. It may minimize tax liability and maximize the benefits afforded under the Tax Code.

4. Through the use of for-profit entities, it may avoid challenges to the involvement of the university, as a tax-exempt entity, in profit-making activities.

5. It provides a convenient vehicle for the management and super-

vision of the research partnership, separate and apart from the regular management of the institution itself.

6. It affords the institution a coherent way to manage and coordinate several different research partnerships, each one organized around a particular research interest and thereby attracting one or more particular commercial partners who are similarly inclined.

The research partnership can itself act as the vehicle for further interrelationships. For example, in addition to the general partners of the commercial entity and the university (through a string of intermediaries), there may also be limited partners whose interest is to invest in the partnership with a view toward sharing in the equity appreciation that will occur if the discoveries are successfully exploited. This infusion of resources in return for a share of the equity can enable the research partnership to more effectively capitalize on its projects. The research partnership may also enter into agreements with other commercial entities, both foreign and domestic, for the further development and commercial exploitation of the discoveries, including their production both at home and abroad.

Rewarding Faculty: Competing with the Private Sector

A very important attribute of this design is its ability to give faculty researchers an incentive to remain with the institution instead of succumbing to the siren song of private enterprise. By allowing faculty to accept a share in the equity of the research partnership, in the form of a limited partnership, the institution can offer the prized faculty member a chance to share in the economic benefits that would accrue from the successful exploitation of his or her discoveries. Because the faculty member would be a limited partner or a shareholder, he or she would be proscribed from involvement in the management of the research partnership, an important component to minimize conflict of interest and disruption of the academic enterprise. In the case of a partnership, since the price paid for transcending this restriction is unlimited liability for its debts and obligations, there is a strong incentive for the faculty member to abide by the rules. This is important because there is always an underlying concern over conflict of interest: Is the faculty member working for the institution or for the research partnership in which he or she has an equity interest?

Confidentiality and Academic Freedom

Closely related to conflict of interest is the question of academic freedom. Colleges and universities pride themselves on being intellectually open. In fact, an increasing number of institutions decline to accept classified governmental research on the grounds that an inability to disclose the fruits of research is inconsistent with the fundamental premises of higher education. But in developing relationships with the commercial sector, confidentiality is a fact of life. Premature disclosure of a discovery can distort the marketplace and cost the commercial partner vast sums. Yet the need to protect the ability of researchers to publish their findings in an appropriate fashion must be preserved as well.

The solution is the use of confidentiality agreements between the institution, commercial partners, and faculty researchers that carefully define what can be released, by whom, and under what circumstances. If such an agreement is entered into at the outset of a research partnership effort, it is relatively easy to protect the varied interests of the parties. But where it is ignored, there is great opportunity for mischief.

Incidentally, it is not uncommon for prospective commercial partners to require faculty researchers to sign their confidentiality agreements, precluding the researchers from using anything they learn from the company but giving the company the right to use whatever it learns from the researcher! This is obviously an undesirable outcome and one that can be avoided by using the institution's own form of agreement.

Creating the Mechanisms: Owning the Tools

Finally, in creating research partnerships, it is essential to consider the manner by which the institution establishes the necessary structures, enters into the appropriate agreements and understandings, and acquires the requisite equipment and facilities. The problem here is only partially substantive; it is also one of state of mind. Many trustees, presidents, and chief financial officers—not to mention deans, department heads, and faculty senates—share a common belief that there is something occult about the business world, some quality beyond the capacity of academics to ponder, let alone control. Typically, academics lapse into a reactive mode, waiting for some commercial concern or venture capitalist to lead the way. But if there is any area in which an institution should itself take the lead, it is in the structuring of these kinds of relationships. Only the institution and its leadership understand the nature of the particular academic enterprise and therefore can tailor a structure to fit the nuances and concerns of that enterprise. More important, however, is that potential commercial partners of venture capitalists have their particular self-interest at stake. That interest may well be similar to the institution's, but it cannot be coextensive. A dollar of revenue or profit that goes to the institution must come from somewhere, and commercial partners or venture capitalists have an obvious—and very natural—interest in seeing that it does not come from their share. Similarly, when it comes to the sharing of risks, commercial partners or venture capitalists must, again quite properly, seek to minimize their own exposure, often at the expense of the institution. This implies several things.

1. The institution must develop its own plans for relationships with the commercial world and have, either in place or fully designed, the necessary structures to accommodate its interests. Such structures might include subsidiary and intermediary entities, management designs, licensing, and confidentiality agreements.

2. Those plans must be developed with the assistance and guidance of experts—lawyers, accountants, and investment bankers—whose only interests lie in serving their client, the institution. Divided loyalties in situations such as these are at best confusing and at worst destined to redound to the great disadvantage of the institution.

3. The institution must be willing to risk some of its own resources to accomplish its goals. There is no free lunch when it comes to the commercial marketplace. Everything has its price. The college administration must be prepared to risk some capital to put itself in a position to make this kind of an effort viable. This is not to say that using other people's money is not desirable. Obviously, quite the contrary is the case. However, the intital resources need to be those of the institution, just as the initial planners need to have undivided loyalty.

The creation of research partnerships affords colleges and universities a unique opportunity to merge their interest in promoting knowledge and serving the public good with developing the substantial resources necessary to enable them to continue to carry out effective programs of research, instruction, and service. Research partnerships are not panaceas. But properly developed, organized, and managed, they can open new avenues for the financial support of the institution and for the better integration of its work with that of society. And, they can do this in a manner consistent with the proper purposes and role of higher education.

Michael B. Goldstein is a partner with the firm of Dow, Lohnes, and Albertson, Washington, D.C.

Many small, private colleges are examining aggressive ways of economically developing their land and other physical assets.

Equity Financing: Real Estate

Richard Thomas, Jonathan Davies

Historically, colleges and universities have carefully managed their financial resources. Investment advisers care for large endowments that are looked on by administrators as a stable source of annual cash flow. Because the administrators rely so heavily on investment income, the portfolio managers have usually adopted a very conservative approach to the selection of investments.

The investment portfolio of most colleges and universities consists of a diversified group of passive securities. These securities generally consist of high-grade stocks, bonds, and other financial instruments that were either received as contributions from donors or purchased with cash available to the university. On occasion, the investment portfolio will contain some real and/or personal property. In most cases, these tangible properties were acquired through a contribution. Often, tangible investment properties are merely leased to third parties in an effort to produce a constant stream of cash flow that may be used by the university to carry out its other functions.

The traditionally conservative investment strategy employed by most colleges and universities has resulted from four independent factors. First, those responsible for the investment of the funds accumulated by colleges and universities have generally adopted a policy of risk avoidance; given the fiduciary duties inherent in serving as a trustee of a tax-exempt entity, most individuals decide to avoid market risks whenever possible.

Second, many colleges and universities have avoided more aggressive investment activities because of their understanding of certain aspects of their tax-exempt status. Most institutions have taken the position that as tax-exempt entities they are prohibited from entering into certain market transactions. Whether a result of state laws controlling the activity of tax-exempt entities or federal rules restricting tax-exempt status, this belief has generally led investment advisers of colleges and universities toward more conservative investments.

Third, most colleges and universities have viewed their investment portfolios as a recurring source of income that may be considered in the annual budgeting process. In an effort to accomplish this objective, portfolio managers have often limited the scope of their investment horizon to the instruments that produce the desired annual stream of income. They have avoided instruments that offer a potentially higher return but a less stable annual cash payment.

Finally, most colleges and universities have traditionally lacked the expertise needed to manage a diversified portfolio that includes investments other than traditional financial instruments. Administrators of colleges and universities generally have the skills necessary to achieve the goals of their institutions. However, few administrators possess the skills needed to participate successfully in a real estate development or venture capital project.

The Need to Diversify

Although this conservative investment strategy has functioned reasonably well in the past, recent political and economic conditions require that it be reevaluated. Most important, higher education institutions need to rethink and expand their concept of assets and total investment strategy.

Clearly, the amount of financial support colleges and universities will be able to obtain from the public sector will diminish in the near future. The budgetary constraints now facing both federal and state governments seem to indicate that colleges and universities will no longer be able to view the public sector as a stable source of annual funding. Therefore, prudent administrators should try to obtain the maximum yield from their investment portfolios.

The reduction of direct public-sector funding appears to be accompanied by a reduction in indirect government funding of colleges and universities. The Tax Reform Act of 1986 reduces both the number of individuals who will be able to obtain a tax benefit as a result of charitable giving (for example, the new tax law eliminates the charitable contribution deduction for nonitemizers) and the dollar value of the benefit available to those who qualify (that is, the new law substantially reduces the marginal tax rate for individuals and corporations and imposes an alternative minimum tax on certain amounts of a charitable contribution).

Assuming that the market reacts rationally to the reduction in the federal subsidy, private contributions to colleges and universities should fall after 1986. Thus, administrators will have another reason to place greater emphasis on the internal generation of funds.

In addition to the reductions in direct and indirect public sector funding, the radical shifts in the economy over the last ten years seem to suggest a shift in the investment strategy of many institutions. The instability in the value of financial assets caused by the inflationary trends of the late 1970s followed by the rapid drop in nominal interest rates experienced in the early 1980s have made it difficult for investment managers to maintain portfolios that produce a relatively constant cash flow in terms of both real and nominal dollars.

As a result of these socioeconomic factors, many investment managers have begun to diversify their portfolios in an effort to optimize over the long term total real wealth available to their universities. This diversification process has included venturing into equity type investment activities that, in the recent past, were not considered an appropriate investment realm for tax-exempt entities. But the recent inflationary period has raised the value of the real assets of these institutions and has forced institutional officers to pay more attention to their management. The real resources of an institution—land and buildings—should be integrated into the overall investment strategy of the institution.

Approaches to Real Estate Investment

The participation of colleges and universities in the real estate market has generally been limited to the management of the facilities actually used by an institution for tax-exempt purposes. When a university received a contribution of real estate, its investment manager usually attempted to convert the real estate into cash available for investment in other securities or a mortgage that would provide the institution with a guaranteed and fixed stream of cash flows.

In certain instances, colleges and universities have been indirect participants in the real estate market. Their participation traditionally consisted of the purchase of a diversified portfolio of mortgage instruments through a secondary market transaction or, in more limited instances, the acquisition of an interest in a direct mortgage loan.

Seldom have colleges and universities sought either contributions of real estate that would be held for more than a short period or opportunities in which available funds could be invested in a real estate project. As a result, colleges and universities have generally forsaken the opportunity to participate in the operating income and/or appreciation available to the owners of real estate. In other words, colleges and universities have generally been willing to forgo the rewards—and risks—of real estate ownership and instead have been willing to place themselves in a position that is no more substantive—and no more risky—than that of a real estate financier.

In the past few years, more and more colleges and universities have demonstrated an interest in acquiring and holding real estate as part of their investment portfolio. To earn investment income more comparable to that of a real estate owner, colleges and universities have begun to pursue vigorously two types of acquisitive transaction.

Real Estate Contributions. Colleges and universities have always placed great emphasis on procuring funds from private sector contributions. Increasingly, however, colleges and universities have sought to have private individuals and corporations make contributions in the form of interests in developed and undeveloped real estate.

One of the most interesting forms of the real estate contribution transaction consists of what has been termed a bargain sale to charity. In bargain sale transactions, the donor transfers property to a university as a contribution but also receives some consideration for the property transferred. Such a bargain sale transaction is particularly desirable in situations where the property that the donor wishes to contribute is encumbered by a mortgage that the donor does not wish to settle currently or where the donor is unwilling to contribute the entire property to the tax-exempt organization.

The donor's inducement to engage in the bargain sale transaction consists of a combination of the consideration that he receives from the university and the tax benefit that he receives from the available charitable contribution deduction. The incentive created by a combination of these inducements can best be demonstrated by the following example.

Individual X purchased a parcel of real estate in 1935 for $35,000. During the next ten years, X improved the real estate through the construction of five buildings at a cost of $150,000. The construction was financed by a mortgage that has a current balance of $75,000. For tax purposes, the improvements to the real estate have been fully depreciated.

In August 1986, X realized that he needed to sell the property quickly to enable him to make certain other investments. The property was appraised at a value of $1,500,000. However, because X needed an immediate sale, he was only able to obtain cash offers of $950,000. If X had sold the property for $950,000, he would have realized $674,800 in cash after taxes under the new law. The calculations for net cash from sale under the new and old laws follows. Because of phase-in provisions in the tax law, the results for the intervening years would fall between these calculations:

	Pre-1987 Tax Law	*Post-1989 Tax Law*
Cash sale price	$950,000	$950,000
Mortgage balance	(75,000)	(75,000)
Federal taxes [($750,000 − $35,000) × Tax Rate]	(143,000)	(200,200)
Net cash from sale	$732,000	$674,800

If X had chosen to donate the property to a tax-exempt entity in exchange for the assumption of the underlying mortgage and $450,000 cash, his after-federal-tax cash proceeds would have been calculated as follows:

	Pre-1987 Tax Law	Post-1989 Tax Law
Cash sale price	$450,000	$450,000
Federal tax [(($450,000 + $75,000) - ($35,000 × $325,000/$1,500,000)) × Tax Rate]	(103,485)	(144,877)
Tax benefit of charitable contribution deduction [($1,500,000 - $325,000) × Tax Rate]	587,500	329,000
Net cash from sale	$934,015	$634,123

In other words, through the bargain sale transaction, X is able to dispose of the property quickly to a charitable organization and to realize almost as high an after-tax cash flow as that which would have been realized from an immediate sale.

As a result of a bargain basement transaction, a university obtains real estate at a cost that is below the current market price. In the example above, the university was able to obtain property with a fair value of $1,500,000 for a total consideration of only $325,000. The university is then free to operate and develop the real estate in the manner that it feels will result in the production of the largest amount of investment income.

Participating Arrangements. In addition to seeking contributions of real estate, colleges and universities that wish to enter into real estate ownership should consider the use of certain types of participation agreements as a method of obtaining some of the benefits of real estate ownership. These participation arrangements generally take one of three forms.

Participating Leases. In many cases, a university will seek to exploit properties by leasing those properties to third parties. The advantages of this system of real estate ownership consist of the following:

1. *Minimization of risk.* By leasing property to a third-party operator, the university accepts little of the financial risk inherent in most real estate projects.

2. *Acquisition of expertise.* Through the lease arrangement, the university is able to transfer the development and management responsibilities to a third party that, hopefully, possesses the expertise needed to exploit the real property.

3. *Participation in residual.* Since the lease generally results in the university retaining the residual interest in the property, any appreciation realized will ultimately be received by the university.

Unfortunately, in a lease arrangement the university trades any right it might have in the operating income produced by the property for a guaranteed fixed rent. Although this trade-off may be prudent in many situations, there are cases in which it would seem desirable for the university to maintain some interest in the current operating income of the project. These situations would include instances in which a long-term lease is negotiated (that is, situations in which the university will not be able to realize a cash residual value for many years) and situations in which a very risky project has the potential for producing large cash flows from operations.

By entering into a participating lease, the university may be able to secure some of the benefits of current operations. In the traditional participating lease, the lessor is guaranteed a minimum fixed annual rent plus a variable participating rent that is determined as a percentage of the annual operating income derived from the property. Thus, while a participating lease allows the university to claim many of the advantages inherent in a lease arrangement (low risk, third-party expertise, residual participation), there is an opportunity to retain a portion of the operating income potential inherent in the property.

Participating Financings. In instances where a university wishes to invest cash in a real estate project, it may seek to structure its investment in the form of a participating loan. Since the university generally cannot benefit from the tax attributes produced as a result of property ownership, an investment structured as a loan with an interest rate that is ultimately tied to the success of the project would be desirable for both the borrower and tax-exempt lender.

A participating loan arrangement would have at least two advantages over a more traditional loan. First, by structuring its investment as a loan, the university can minimize the risk associated with an investment in real estate. Since a lender's rights are generally superior to those of equity owners, the university that invests through a loan is able to retain for itself a priority in liquidation that is superior to that of other investors. This priority may become important if the project ultimately proves to be a failure.

Second, through a participating loan, the university is able to retain some of the attributes of property ownership. Most participating loans provide for a fixed interest rate plus an "equity kicker" that is a function of the profitability of the project being financed. The equity kicker may be paid annually (based on operating results), at the date of ultimate sale of the property (based on net residual value), or at a fixed date (based on the appraised value of the property). Regardless of the structure of the equity kicker, the university should realize from successful projects a higher rate of return than that which would have been realized had the institution merely participated in a more traditional real estate loan.

Joint Venture Participations. In many cases, a university may find it desirable to participate directly as a real estate joint venture. Such joint ventures may be structured as tenancies in common, partnerships, or corporations. However, in the past, federal income tax considerations have resulted in most real estate joint ventures being structured as partnerships.

In a traditional joint venture, a university-investor would exchange cash for a true interest in the real estate project. Such an investment results in the tax-exempt entity obtaining a true interest in all of the beneficial attributes of the real estate investment and all the risks associated with that venture. Although the risks may be reduced if the university acquires either a limited partnership interest or corporate stock, two facts should be considered with respect to such investments.

First, the ownership of corporate stock or a limited partnership interest does not limit the degree to which the initial investment of the joint venturer is at risk. If the project is an ultimate failure, the limited partner or corporate stockholder has little or no priority with respect to the return of the initial investment.

Second, the ownership of corporate stock or a limited partnership interest substantially restricts the degree of control that the investor may exercise over the project. Limited partners are generally precluded from exercising control over the business of the partnership. Corporate stockholders have the ability to elect directors of the corporation but seldom have any direct control over day-to-day business decisions. This lack of control constitutes a significant risk inherent in any such real estate investment.

A Caveat. The above discussion clearly indicates that a participation in a real estate project may be advantageous for a university. However, any institution considering such an investment should realize that the receipt of a participation in the benefits of real estate ownership involves certain risks and trade-offs.

To obtain a participation, the university will generally have to relinquish some of the guaranteed rights that would traditionally have been received. It is not uncommon for a participating interest to be offered only in exchange for a reduction in fixed interest and/or rent payments. In addition, it is not uncommon for a participation to be accompanied by a reduction in the legal recourse available to the participating investor.

In analyzing such arrangements, a university must consider the necessary trade-offs within the context of its own organizational goals. To make such an analysis, the university must have the equivalent of a comprehensive business plan that fully describes overall investment objectives, acceptable degrees of risk, and minimum levels of required return.

Tax Problems Inherent in Equity Investments

In the last year, the private sector and business community have become increasingly sensitive to the participation of tax-exempt entities in what have been traditionally viewed as for-profit activities. In mid-September, the House Ways and Means Committee announced that it would conduct hearings to investigate whether the laws concerning the tax exemption granted to certain institutions should be modified to reflect their more vigorous participation in for-profit activities.

The vocalization of the business community's increased sensitivity and announcement of hearings in the House of Representatives seems to confirm a belief that tax practitioners have held for several years: The participation of tax-exempt entities in areas that have been traditionally the province of taxable business entities raises serious public policy questions concerning the proper application of current federal tax laws. The more specific concern of tax practitioners has generally been concentrated on four specific tax issues.

Tax-Exempt Status. To be exempt from federal income taxes, an organization must establish that its principal purpose and primary activities are to promote certain not-for-profit, socially desirable functions. If the principal purpose or primary activity of a university changes, that entity could lose its tax-exempt status.

Given the magnitude of certain real estate transactions, it is possible that some tax-exempt participants could jeopardize their tax-exempt status by becoming substantial investors. If tax-exempt status were lost, all the income of the organization could be subject to tax, and donors to the organization would no longer be entitled to a federal tax deduction for contributions.

To avoid this potential problem, many colleges and universities have formed for-profit corporate subsidiaries to invest in certain noncharitable activities. Although the income derived from these corporate subsidiaries is generally used by the tax-exempt organization to promote nonprofit goals, the corporate subsidiaries are subject to federal taxation in the same manner as other for-profit entities. However, the presence of the for-profit subsidiary generally protects the university from the potential revocation of its tax-exempt federal tax status.

Unrelated Trade or Business Income. As colleges and universities enter into ventures that have traditionally been undertaken by for-profit entities, these institutions run the risk of having the income from their participation taxed as unrelated trade or business income (UTBI). Although many types of income are specifically excluded from the definition of UTBI (royalties, rents, interest, among others), many types of income realized as a result of an entity's participation in a real estate development may be classified as UTBI (for example, profits from the resale of development sites or profits from the operation of a hotel).

If a tax-exempt entity has UTBI, that income will be taxed in the same manner as the income of a for-profit entity. However, if the UBTI is deemed to be debt financed, certain modified rules will be applied to make it more likely that the tax-exempt entity will actually pay a tax as a result of its participation in the for-profit activity.

Assuming that a tax-exempt entity realizes income from its real estate investments, there appear to be three ways to avoid having that income considered UTBI. First, the tax-exempt entity could attempt to prove that the real estate income falls into one of the classes that is exempt from tax under the Internal Revenue Code. Exempt classes of income are specifically defined and generally construed in a narrow manner.

Second, the tax-exempt entity could attempt to prove that the source of the real estate income is somehow related to its tax-exempt purpose. In other words, the entity could argue that its participation in the real estate investment was actually a simple extension of its tax-exempt purpose. In general, the IRS has been quite liberal in their application of this exception to the UTBI rules.

Finally, the tax-exempt entity could attempt to avoid UTBI by arguing that the real estate activity in which it participates is not a trade or business. For federal income tax purposes, a trade or business is an activity that is conducted for profit or on a regular and recurring basis. If the real estate profits of the tax-exempt entity are derived from a one-time activity, it may be possible to argue that the entity is not engaged in a trade or business and therefore is not subject to UTBI rules.

Step Transaction Doctrine. Under the step transaction doctrine, the Internal Revenue Service has the right to tax a series of related transactions as a single transaction if it can be established that the intent of the parties was truly to consummate the single transaction. The most easily understood situation in which the step transaction doctrine would apply consists of a contribution of appreciated property followed by a sale of that property by the tax-exempt entity. If the transaction were viewed as a direct sale of that property followed by a contribution of the proceeds to the tax-exempt entity, the donor would be required to pay tax on the gain inherent in the property. Thus, the economics of the transaction would change substantially for the donor.

Whenever a university participates in a series of transactions, the possible application of the step transaction doctrine must be considered. Although it is possible that the application of the doctrine will have little or no effect on the underlying transaction, it is also possible that the economic impact of the application of the step transaction doctrine would be massive.

To avoid the application of the step transaction doctrine, the university and the other participants in the investment transaction must make sure that the substance of the transaction does not deviate from the form selected for implementing the transaction. If the form and substance of a transaction are in parity, the IRS will generally be precluded from applying the step transaction doctrine.

Tax-Exempt Entity Leasing. In the early 1980s, a number of for-profit organizations began to enter into significant transactions with tax-exempt entities. These transactions were generally designed to use the federal tax status of the tax-exempt entities to produce a tax shelter for the for-profit entities.

In 1984 Congress enacted legislation specifically designed to deal with this potential abuse. Although the legislation addresses transactions structured as partnerships, operating agreements, and leases, the rules have generally been termed the tax-exempt entity leasing rules.

The tax-exempt entity leasing rules are designed to preclude a transfer of tax benefits from a tax-exempt entity that cannot use those benefits to a taxable entity that can use them. The rules have little or no effect on tax-exempt participants in transactions. However, the application of these rules can have a significant effect on the after-tax returns that can be realized by for-profit entities that engage in transactions with tax-exempt entities.

The tax-exempt entity rules are quite complex—far beyond the scope of this chapter. Yet it is important that colleges and universities contemplating equity investments be aware of the presence of these rules and how they can affect a specific transaction.

Summary

The changing conditions in both the public and private sectors will force colleges and universities to reevaluate their overall investment strategy. Many such entities will find it advantageous to enter into certain equity investments that would not have been considered in the past. The nature of these new investments can range from direct ownership of tangible property to joint and participating ownership arrangements consisting of leases, financings, and partnerships. Although these new investment vehicles may provide increased returns to colleges and universities, the potential tax consequences should be considered.

Richard Thomas is president of Pennfield Corporation, a subsidiary of Mercer University.

Jonathan Davies is a tax partner in the firm of Coopers & Lybrand.

Tax reform increases the need for integrated financial planning of nontraditional income-generating activities and of capital sources and uses.

Making It All Work: Sound Financial Management

William F. Massy

The Tax Reform Act of 1986 creates a need for integrated financial planning by colleges and universities. Planning for nontraditional income-generating activities and for sources and uses of capital for academic programs is particularly important, yet the state of the art is largely undeveloped in higher education. Most work is oriented toward financial planning for current academic operations or deals with specific projects.

This chapter considers nontraditional income sources and then provides a paradigm for integrating capital with other financial needs, with particular attention to the impact of tax reform. Throughout this examination, it must be remembered that colleges and universities are significant business entities and should be managed as such. On the other hand, colleges and universities are educational institutions; this is their reason for being and the underpinning of their political and fund-raising support.

Financial planning for operations has become routine in higher education. The planning process and associated financial forecasting models developed at Stanford University in the early 1970s, as reported by Hopkins and Massy (1981), were adopted by many institutions. Although this type of financial planning model covers current operations well, it lacks detailed treatment of nontraditional income opportunities and sources and uses of capital for academic programs.

R. E. Anderson, J. W. Meyerson (eds.). *Financing Higher Education: Strategies After Tax Reform.*
New Directions for Higher Education, no. 58. San Francisco: Jossey-Bass, Summer 1987.

Nontraditional Income Opportunities

There are two kinds of opportunities: (1) those directly related to the academic purpose of a college or university, such as the sale or licensing of intellectual property; and (2) activities not so related, such as land development or sale of nonacademic services to outside users. Goldstein (this volume) describes the former and Thomas and Davies (this volume) discuss the latter.

The nontraditionalist entrepreneur views a college or university as a business conglomerate that attempts to exploit its assets and operating strengths according to market opportunities. Creation of a for-profit subsidiary to seek out and exploit market opportunities for the benefit of the school's teaching and research program may be a logical or even necessary outgrowth of this philosophy.

Tax reform and other political decisions affecting higher education will increase the pressure to exploit nontraditional income opportunities as well as changing the rules of the game. Colleges and universities may have a comparative advantage in certain business activities (for example, through synergy with academic operations or provision of financial liquidity and "patient" capital). Concern has been expressed, however, that vigorous pursuit of nontraditional income will distract academic leaders, warp institutional priorities, dilute goodwill, and eventually erode political support for higher education as a whole. Whether this is true, and whether for-profit subsidiaries will mitigate this risk, should be the subject of serious discussion.

Sources and Uses of Capital for Academic Purposes

"To make it all work," a comprehensive review of the capital sources and uses and an assessment of the forces that act on them is necessary. Tax reform will make capital more expensive, thus placing a premium on balancing capital needs against operating expenditures. It will also make it more difficult for many parents to accumulate savings to pay tuition, which will increase price competition among higher education institutions.

Uses of Capital. Higher education has become a capital-intensive industry, and capital requirements are growing. The needs, and the reasons for growth, are as follows:

1. *Facilities construction and renovation.* Education and research in science, technology, and medicine depend on increasingly sophisticated and expensive laboratory buildings. In addition, many facilities at colleges and universities are wearing out (Kaiser in this volume describes these problems in detail). (See also National Science Board and others, 1986).

2. *Equipment.* The need for teaching and research equipment par-

allels that for facilities, and programs for productivity improvement in administration and support services require more information processing and telecommunications equipment.

3. *Housing for faculty and staff.* Many institutions must provide rental housing or special mortgage loans to faculty and staff members to mitigate recruiting and retention problems. House prices and rents are going up in many parts of the country, which inflates the importance of these programs.

4. *Student loans.* Direct loans to students or parents are needed in order to maintain affordability and the institution's competitive position in the face of rising real tuition rates.

5. *Working capital.* Tuition deferral plans, slower payment of research and Medicare obligations by the federal government, and the general stretch-out in trade receivables caused by high real interest rates are raising working capital requirements.

6. *Endowment and other investments.* Pressures on operating income and expenses require greater reliance on investment income. The accumulation of investment funds represents an important use of capital. Diversification of investments into new kinds of vehicles raises expected return in relation to risk. Tax reform makes equity real estate a better candidate for diversification of tax-exempt investment funds (as discussed by Thomas and Davies in this volume).

Sources of Capital. Gifts and government support once were the traditional sources of capital for colleges and universities. Access to these has been restricted in recent years, however, and it has become necessary to consider new options. What follows is a summary of the alternatives that are available at the present time.

1. *Retention from operations.* Unrestricted or unrestricted-designated funds may be retained from current operations by running surpluses or making nonmandatory transfers to plant, quasi-endowment, student loans, or reserves for contingencies. Transfers for funding depreciation fall into this category as well. Price competition will limit increases in tuition and the full recovery of costs on sponsored research programs, thus placing greater pressure on operating budgets and inhibiting capital transfers.

2. *Accounts payable and receipt of prepayments.* Accounts payable can be managed to minimize use of cash and prepayments may be sought from students, foundations, and government when conditions are favorable.

3. *Gifts and foundation grants.* Institutions rely heavily on individuals and foundations for endowment capital and facilities construction. The funds may be restricted or unrestricted, but they are always regarded as equity capital because the provider views them as an investment in the institution rather than procurement of a service. There is, of course, no obligation for repayment.

4. *Government grants and contracts.* Once a major source of capital

for facilities, most federal grants and contracts for research now restrict expenditures to support of current operations and, to a limited extent, the purchase of equipment. Efforts to provide capital to institutions directly through the political process, without scientific peer group review, are being resisted by most members of the higher education community on grounds that such measures fail to allocate resources to maximize scientific productivity.

5. *Research partnerships and other arrangements with private industry.* This is an area of growing potential for both capital funding and operating support. Goldstein (this volume) describes the R & D partnership, an important vehicle that gains impetus from tax reform. Stanford's Center for Integrated Systems and its Technology Licensing Program provide other examples of what can be accomplished. The approach is not without problems, however, since industry support may involve conflicts of interest or raise questions of intellectual property rights that may run counter to deeply held scientific values.

6. *State and local government programs.* Public institutions have access to capital from their sponsoring agencies. Eligible uses and terms vary enormously, as does availability.

7. *Debt.* Borrowing by colleges and universities has mushroomed during the last fifteen years because of the decline in federal funding for facilities, capital needs for student loan and faculty-staff housing programs, and the increased availability of tax-exempt financing. Kaiser (this volume) gives statistics about the fraction of academic facilities being financed nationwide by debt.

8. *Leasing.* Capital or operating leases can be used to finance facilities and equipment without incurring debt, and this kind of financing is expected to grow. Tax-exempt capital leases are available as substitutes for tax-exempt bonds, as described by Eden (this volume). Leasing should be treated as debt rather than as equity for purposes of capital planning.

The Integrated Financing Plan

Two elements are required for an integrated financial plan: (1) All the important sources and uses of capital must be considered together, and (2) the impacts of alternative capital funding strategies on the school's operating budget must be evaluated.

Many colleges and universities plan for specific types of capital sources and uses. Comprehensive facilities plans are becoming more common, for example, and capital requirements are projected for student loans and housing programs. Fund-raising campaigns include goals for facilities and for endowment to support particular programs or the general needs of the institution. But few institutions try to bring these matters together into a single comprehensive plan.

The following example of integrated financial planning is based on existing models at Stanford. Although much remains to be accomplished, this model outlines the beginnings of an integrated financial plan.

Financial Planning for Operations. Projections of the income and expenses attributable to current operations and investment activities form the cornerstone of the integrated financial plan. At Stanford, these are brought together in the long-range financial forecast, which is presented to the trustees and the faculty senate during each year's budgeting cycle.

The forecasting process starts with an assessment of economic activity, inflation, wage rates, and interest rates over a three-year period. Income and expense trends are projected by the responsible line officers, aided by the university budget staff. These projections inform decision makers about policy parameters such as tuition, salary growth, the transfer to plant, the amount of income to be withheld for later allocation in the conditional budget, and the aggregate amount of budget cutting and funding for new programs. The proximate year's forecast evolves into a set of budget guidelines as the year progresses, with the out-years being updated frequently to conform to changes in the current budget base. Decisions about specific line items of budget authority must conform to the overall budget guidelines for the year. Allocation of the conditional budget takes place as the need arises and is completed at year-end closing. This process has been in place at Stanford since the mid 1970s (Hopkins and Massy, 1981).

Tax reform is likely to hurt Stanford's long-range financial situation by inhibiting gifts to support current operations and raising the cost of pensions, interest charges, and student financial aid needed to compensate for taxation of stipends over and above tuition and necessary equipment. Although not all of these effects may turn out to be important, the overall effects could be significant. We do not believe we differ from other private institutions in this respect.

Tax reform will make college less affordable, as Hart points out (this volume). The loss of Clifford Trusts and similar tax-shelter mechanisms makes it much more difficult to accumulate money to pay tuition—especially as tuition continues to grow in real terms. Newly proposed tuition prepayment plans offer only a partial solution to the affordability problem. The following issues arise in connection with these "tuition futures" plans.

1. *The problem of student choice.* Will the range of alternative educational opportunities be narrowed prematurely?
2. *Tax treatment.* Under what conditions will accumulations under the plans be free of tax?
3. *Risk sharing and institutional autonomy.* To what extent will it be necessary for institutions to relinquish the authority to set future tuition rates and will they do so?

The last problem will be particularly severe for private institutions, which cannot rely on state appropriations to make up any tuition shortfalls. Stanford is not considering such a plan.

Academic Facilities Planning. Tax reform will also affect the funds available for academic facilities. The main sources for funds at Stanford are (1) the facilities reserve (funded by transfers from the current division to the plant division), (2) gifts (mostly from living individuals), and (3) long-term debt. In addition, capital is sometimes provided by research sponsors. Stanford used a form of off-balance-sheet financing for its cogeneration plant but did not find other circumstances where this was appropriate.

Stanford will soon announce a fund-raising campaign to commemorate its centennial. Planning for the campaign began with an assessment of needs and the identification and rating of prospects. The provost allocates access to fund-raising prospects, just as he allocates cash from the facilities reserve. The allocation process encompasses endowment and current program support as well as funding for facilities. It is based on the assumption that good prospects are scarce resources and that access to them should be determined according to institutional priorities.

Tax reform will subject a portion of large gifts to the alternative minimum tax. The impact of this could be substantial. In addition, some private institutions (including Stanford) will lose access to tax-exempt bonds.

Debt outstanding for academic facilities at Stanford has grown from $10 million in 1980 to $103 million today. (Total debt outstanding, including that for auxiliaries and bank lines, exceeds $300 million.) Debt service for academic facilities has grown from 1.1 percent of the operating budget to 3.25 percent over the same period. This trend led, two years ago, to the development of trustee policy guidelines for the permissible amount of debt and debt service for academic facilities. The new policy limits debt service to 5 percent of the operating budget and the growth of debt service to an incremental 0.75 percent per annum on a three-year moving average basis. (Previously, the goal had been simply to minimize use of debt, considering it as a last resort on a case-by-case basis.) The new policy aims to prevent current program needs from mortgaging future needs and to protect Stanford's AAA credit rating. The effect is to require the allocation of a fixed amount of future debt among contending projects.

The planning process for academic facilities now seeks to integrate the aforementioned three allocations: cash, fund-raising potential, and debt. This substantially increases planning discipline by forcing consideration of project priorities in the context of a unified set of funding possibilities, all with clearly identified size limits.

Debt Structure Planning. Stanford's financing strategy has been to use long-term tax-exempt bonds when borrowing for academic facilities and bank credit lines to finance equipment, working capital, and, where applicable, student loans. Tax reform will deny tax-exempt debt to private institutions, including Stanford, with more than $150 million of such debt outstanding. The looming threat to tax-exempt financing and an immediate need to finance faculty-staff housing programs led, in 1986, to Stanford's first taxable bond issue in many years. The experience precipitated a decision to rationalize our overall debt structure.

Long-term taxable financing means accessing the corporate bond market, which differs significantly from the municipal bond market in which tax-exempt issues are floated. First, the enabling laws usually require that tax-exempt financing be linked to specific projects and amortized over the useful life of those projects. No such limitations exist in the corporate market. Second, there are timing rules for spending tax-exempt bond proceeds and strict limits on arbitrage, neither of which apply to taxable issues. Third, maturities of twenty-five to thirty years are the rule in the municipals market, whereas ten or fifteen years is considered long in the corporate market. Fourth, it is possible to act much more quickly in the corporate market because no state approvals are required for a taxable issue; however, note that Securities and Exchange Commission rules may apply. Fifth, there may be more flexibility in managing a corporate offering, since many states have strict underwriting rules (or even short lists of eligible firms) for bonds issued through their tax-exempt authorities. Finally, of course, tax-exempt bonds traditionally sell at 150 to 200 basis points below treasury bonds of equivalent maturity, whereas high-quality corporate bonds sell at 50 basis points or more over treasuries. (See Clapp's chapter in this volume for a comprehensive description of the differences between the taxable and municipal markets.)

The differences between corporate and municipal markets offer a new approach to managing an institution's debt structure. The shorter maturities in the corporate market will require that increments of debt be rolled over before they are fully amortized. Elimination of the need to tie borrowing to specific projects makes it possible to uncouple the timing of borrowing from that of project planning by pooling an institution's facilities debt. To add borrowing for working capital, student loans, and other purposes to a debt pool requires little additional effort. The result could be a consolidated institutional credit account, managed to optimize interest rates in relation to maturities and cash flow needs. This account could be optimized jointly with the asset mix in working capital and endowment pools, thus to some extent mitigating the financial consequences of the loss of tax-exempt financing.

Stanford is taking the first steps to set up a consolidated credit account for certain types of new borrowing and is just now working through the implications of this method for financial reporting, accounting for restricted funds, and the allowability of interest on federal grants and contracts. Stanford's financial adviser, L. F. Rothschild Unterberg Towbin, is examining the European and American markets for short- and long-term maturities. The Stanford staff is developing a set of guidelines and a model for managing the maturity structure of Stanford's debt portfolio. These techniques have been used by corporate treasurers for years, but they are new to higher education.

Considerations in Capital Planning

Developing integrated capital plans demands a more careful consideration of the interactions among capital cost, debt-equity ratios for projects, and academic program alternatives. The integration of capital and operating budgets requires a fundamental reexamination of the linkages between financial and programmatic decisions. Tax reform provides an impetus for integration. So does the onset of tuition futures plans.

Cost of Capital. The true cost of capital for alternative financing approaches is measured by three different yardsticks.

1. *Direct dollar costs:* (1) the cost of interest and debt issuance for borrowed capital, net of any indirect cost recovery; (2) the loss of investment return for equity capital; (3) the out-of-pocket cost of acquiring gifts; and (4) the net cost of leasing or other off-balance-sheet financing. These effects are relatively easy to measure, and they are an immediate consideration in comparing alternative sources of capital.

2. *Induced direct effects:* (1) opportunity losses to academic budgets due to interest payments; (2) higher indirect cost rates due to interest payments and the resulting effect on competitiveness in the sponsored research area; (3) using up debt capacity and the resulting possibility of higher borrowing costs for future projects; and (4) using the potential of gift prospects who might otherwise be interested in funding other projects or adding to endowment. Despite their great significance, these effects are often ignored because they are hard to quantify.

3. *Other consequences for present or future activities:* (1) restrictions on the use of gift, grant, or contract funds; (2) regulations pertaining to the use of facilities funded by government agencies or with tax-exempt bonds; (3) limitations on arbitrage with proceeds from tax-exempt bonds; (4) restrictive covenants in loan agreements, such as on the ratio of available funds to liabilities; (5) facilities usage or other limitations in lease agreements; and (6) distortion of teaching and research priorities, confrontations with the academic culture, or assumption of risk associated with nontraditional income-generating activities. Many of these difficulties will be known at the time the capital is acquired, but they may be overshadowed by the immediate pressure to fund the project in question.

Formal planning protocols are needed to track the consequences of using alternative sources of income and capital. Ineffective tracking invites undue concentration on the direct, short-run dollar costs of funding, which opens the way for unpleasant surprises in the future. Tax reform changes the rules of the game to the point where intuitive decision making may become ineffective, thus enhancing the value of integrated planning.

Equity or Debt Financing? Business firms employ debt in order to leverage the earning power of equity. So too with colleges and universities: Use of debt leverages the degree to which equity assets can support academic programs. Leverage permits the construction of more academic and support facilities sooner than would be the case if the capital budget were to be limited by the accumulation of equity funds through transfers to plant or fund-raising in advance of project approval. Leverage can also help equipment acquisitions programs. Many institutions purchase equipment through revolving funds that are financed with external debt. Tax-exempt and conventional leasing have the general characteristics of debt, as pointed out by Eden (this volume).

The choice between debt and equity hinges on (1) the institution's cost of borrowing and return on investing, (2) the degree to which it is willing to accept the risk of leverage, and (3) its time preference or "impatience factor" for academic programs. Higher interest rates for funds invested while awaiting commitment to a capital project will make equity financing more attractive, other things being equal, because the accumulation period is shortened. Conversely, lower interest rates will make debt more attractive. Raising the time preference or impatience factor will also tilt the decision toward debt, which allows program benefits to begin immediately.

The negative impact of tax reform on charitable giving is likely to increase the effective cost of equity capital, which will tend to favor debt. The new limits on arbitrage and the loss of tax-exempt financing for some institutions will offset this to some extent. On balance, though, tax reform favors the use of debt, thus driving up leverage ratios and increasing financial risk.

Risk is the dark side of leverage, because leverage amplifies the effects of contractions in revenue or increases in operating expense. The amount of long-term debt held by colleges and universities has increased dramatically during the past ten years; thus, the risk of leverage is greater than it used to be. In addition, a large amount of debt raises questions of intergenerational equity, because the burden of debt service may fall disproportionately on future cohorts of students and faculty. Tax reform is likely to exacerbate these problems. Long-term tuition guarantees, implicit in the tuition futures plans discussed so far, also increase the effective amount of leverage.

It is useful to contrast the risks of financial leverage in colleges and universities with the more familiar kinds of risk experienced by business firms.

1. Leverage affects the volatility of business profits and the price of the company's stock. Both of these effects manifest themselves quickly. Takeover, merger, or bankruptcy are possible in the longer term.

Leverage decreases the stability of budget-base funding for colleges and universities. "Start-stop" budgeting can be traumatic for an institution, but financial failure is usually not a serious danger. The effects of moderate leverage can be mitigated through utilization of reserves and the cushioning effect of nonmandatory transfers (or in Stanford's case, the conditional budget). These mitigations should not be allowed to produce an undue sense of security about larger amounts of leverage, however.

2. Business firms are guided by capital market conditions in setting their time and risk preference factors, which together with the costs of borrowing and raising equity capital determine the firm's leverage ratio. Although the guidance is inexact, the fact that outcomes are denominated in dollar terms means that the feedback loops are relatively well defined and fast acting.

In contrast, the time and risk factors for colleges and universities are determined on the basis of subjective value judgments, which are not disciplined by the buying and selling of stock in some academic capital market. Although it is true that the institution must eventually come to terms with its markets for students, research sponsors, and faculty, the feedback loops are ill defined and slow to react. (In other words, the markets are quite imperfect.) The institution must discipline itself to avoid impatience, too much tolerance for risk, and warping of academic priorities—all three of which destabilize its budgets and mortgage the academic prospects of future generations of students and faculty.

3. Both equity and debt financing are almost always available to healthy business firms, although their prices will vary over time. Although colleges and universities usually have access to debt financing, this is not necessarily the case for additions to equity—especially for projects without much fund-raising appeal. Without gift potential or nontraditional sources of capital (such as from land development or research partnerships), an equity-financing strategy usually requires a long lead time for the accumulation of resources. The disproportionate lead times for equity and debt financing magnify the importance of the institution's impatience factor. In this respect, the borrowing decision is more like that of consumers than business firms. The prospect of using debt for the immediate gratification of academic program objectives also raises the specter that these objectives may not be as well seasoned as objectives that have withstood the test of time during an equity-capital accumulation period. This is a straw man to some extent, since already-accumulated equity funds may also be spent on unseasoned proposals. On the other hand, an unseasoned proposal funded with debt may result in a situation where the priority of the program fades before the debt has been paid off—a painful outcome that most institutions would like to avoid.

Leverage is a central consideration in financial planning. Care must be taken to avoid reacting to sudden changes in the economic environment, such as tax reform, in ways that will destabilize the institution or reduce its time horizon. A sharp and sustained increase in debt financing for academic facilities or lease arrangements with similar characteristics could do just that. So could an uncritical plunge into nontraditional activities. An integrated financial plan that deals with risk as well as expected benefits, in both the long and short run, is needed.

Effects of the Tax Reform Act of 1986

The consequences of tax reform will not be known for a long time, and it would be presumptuous to attempt precise predictions about its effects on higher education. The following is a general summary and assessment, based partly on other chapters in this book and partly on Stanford's institutional resources.

General Effects. The tax law favors consumption rather than investment, with disproportionate benefits accruing to higher-income individuals not currently making heavy use of tax shelters. This should help some parents' ability to pay for higher education, and it may also be an impetus for charitable giving by some individuals. The law also is likely to increase the total return on college and university investment portfolios, which do not depend on tax shelters and tend to be invested in financial assets rather than real estate. Real estate capitalization rates will drop when and if taxes are raised in order to reduce the federal deficit. Higher tax rates would also provide greater incentives for charitable giving.

The general provisions of the new tax law are likely to hurt colleges and universities in at least two ways. First, the new law is likely to be revenue reducing rather than revenue neutral, despite protestations to the contrary. Lower tax revenues will add to the pressure for budget cuts in which higher education will share at least proportionately. Second, the drop in marginal tax rates will raise the effective price of charitable giving for both individuals and corporations, which will probably reduce the total amount of such giving. Elimination of the nonitemizer deduction will have a similar effect. Finally, the impact of tax reform on the affordability of higher education may well result in a proliferation of tuition futures plans of varying quality and acceptability. This, in turn, exposes higher education to the dangers of balkanized student choice and political intervention.

In the last analysis, the financial health of colleges and universities depends on the health of the economy. The law seems likely to have a modest negative effect on the economy over the next year or so. Washington is betting that tax reform will improve economic performance over the long run, however, because capital will be allocated more efficiently.

Provisions Specific to Higher Education. The Tax Reform Act of

1986 has many provisions that apply specifically to higher education, especially to private colleges and universities. The literature is full of commentary about them, so I shall provide only a brief summary of the most important provisions.

1. *Charitable gifts.* The amount of untaxed appreciation claimed as a deduction is a preference item under the alternative minimum tax.

The effect of the minimum tax on large gifts is unknown but could be significant. There are reports that more than half the donations to higher education since 1983, in dollar amounts, have been in the form of appreciated property. Large gifts are especially important for financing facilities and for additions to endowment.

2. *Tax-exempt bonds.* Section 501(c)(3) bonds, used by private colleges and universities where authorized by state law, were not subjected to a state volume cap as originally planned. Indeed, they were declared for the first time to be private in purpose. On the other hand, the maximum amount of such bonds that a university may have outstanding is $150 million. (Hospital bonds and the proceeds of one refinancing are excluded from the cap, and some institutions were able to obtain transition rules.) Issuance costs above 2 percent may no longer be financed as part of a tax-exempt issue. Interest on 501(c)(3) bonds is not subject to the alternative minimum tax, but the rules governing arbitrage by issuing institutions have been tightened significantly. The same principles appear to apply to tax-exempt leasing.

The effects of these changes will be particularly significant for the approximately twenty large private institutions that are subject to the volume cap. Their cost of debt financing will rise by 100 to 150 basis points, they will be blocked from maturities in excess of about fifteen years for new issues, and their ability to refund existing debt will be limited. Small private institutions will have a difficult time because they have fewer opportunities to adapt to the changed rules of issuance and refunding. Public universities, on the other hand, will continue to have their normal access to tax-exempt financing. The restrictions on arbitrage will raise the cost of capital projects for all institutions.

3. *Scholarships and fellowships.* The amount of any scholarship or fellowship in excess of tuition and required equipment will be considered taxable income to the student.

This provision will produce hardship for many graduate students, and financial aid budgets may have to be raised to offset the tax. Many research and teaching assistants at Stanford will pay taxes of $1,000 or more, and it could cost several million dollars a year to fully immunize them. Differences in tuition rates between public and private institutions do not enter into this equation because tuition grants remain fully exempt from tax.

4. *Interest deductibility on loans for education.* Interest deductibility

is denied on consumer loans, including those to finance education, but it is maintained on home equity loans for education.

The provision concerning home equity loans for education will be important to families straining to afford college. Denial of deductibility for other interest will reduce the demand for loans to parents by colleges and universities and increase tuition resistance and price competition. The effect on government-backed loans will be minimized because they are targeted toward lower-income families. A similar effect is expected to favor loans from other sources that are made to students rather than parents.

5. *Pensions.* The coverage and nondiscrimination rules of Section 401(a) of the Internal Revenue Code are applied to Section 501(c)(3) plans of colleges and universities for the first time. Basically, all employees will have to be considered on a uniform basis in determining whether retirement plans meet the rules. It will be possible to have more than one plan, but the plans will have to meet tests of comparability promulgated by the Treasury Department. Salary reduction components of retirement programs will not be included in the comparability test, but they are subject to the new limit on deferred income. Plans that fail to meet the tests will lose their ability to tax shelter contributions and investment earnings. The new law also imposes a cap of $9,500 on elective contributions made under tax-sheltered annuities and severely limits all kinds of deferred compensation in higher education.

The pension provision's impact on higher education cannot be predicted until the legislative history of the tax law is available, and the situation will not really be clarified until the implementing regulations are written. Colleges and universities have traditionally considered faculty to be in a category by itself. Whether this will be recognized by the regulations remains to be seen. If there is no recognition, which seems to be the most likely outcome, the financial consequences for many private institutions would be significant.

6. *Employee educational assistance and faculty housing.* (1) The exclusion of educational assistance from income is extended through 1987 with a cap of $5,250; (2) exclusion of tuition remission for research and teaching assistants is also extended; and (3) the value of faculty housing is excluded from income if the rent paid to the institution is greater than or equal to 5 percent of the appraised value of the housing.

These provisions are basically favorable to colleges and universities, although the cap on assistance and the 5 percent rule may cause hardship in some cases.

7. *R & D tax credit.* (1) The tax credit to firms that increase their R & D expenditures is extended to the end of 1988 at a rate of 20 percent; (2) there is also a 20 percent credit (reduced by certain factors) for firms giving cash contributions to university basic research; and (3) current law allowing charitable deductions for donations of scientific research equip-

ment is extended to include certain tax-exempt scientific research organizations in addition to universities.

These provisions are also favorable to colleges and universities. Goldstein (this volume) states that the law is expected to enhance significantly the attractiveness of research partnerships.

The Differential Effects on Public and Private Institutions. Tax reform will further tilt the playing field against private colleges and universities, both large and small, as they compete with their public counterparts. The biggest direct effects are likely to be in the areas of charitable giving, tax-exempt bonds, and pension expenses. The first two will affect private institutions disproportionately and the latter focuses on them exclusively. In the end, despite integrated financial planning, tax reform will adversely affect their tuition and indirect cost rates relative to those of public institutions—a relationship that already is strongly influenced by subsidies to the public sector. This will take place in the context of greater tuition resistance by parents and price competition among institutions.

The terms of competition between public and private institutions should greatly concern everyone who values plurality in higher education and seeks to protect the financial health of the many fine schools in both sectors.

The private nonprofit sector is deeply rooted in American culture. As John G. Simon (1979, p. 1) said, "Nonprofit organizations in our society undertake missions that are, in other countries, committed to business enterprises or to the state. Here, we importantly, if not exclusively, rely on the third sector to cure us, to entertain us, to teach us, to study us, to preserve our culture, to defend our rights and the balance of nature, and ultimately to bury us."

The private sector in higher education is uniquely important, despite the fact that public and private colleges and universities are alike in many respects. The power of the case is well described by Robert Rosenzweig, executive director of the Association of American Universities (1985, p. 302), in terms of a paradox.

> The more alike public and private universities become in their functions, and even in the source of their funding, the more important it is to retain a strong set of institutions whose distance from direct political control can enable them to act strongly on behalf of all universities when governments threaten important values in pursuit of some immediate purpose.
>
> The most important word in the last sentence is the adverb: "when," not "if," governments threaten important values. It has happened before; it will inevitably happen again. For reasons of prudence as well as politics, govern-

ments respond to what happens to be urgent, and woe unto what seems less urgent if it stands in the way.

This is no hypothetical concern or nameless fear, and when it occurs, private institutions are in a better position to respond expeditiously. This is surely not because their leaders are braver or more virtuous. Rather, it is because their governing boards are nonpolitical, their core funding tends to be nongovernmental, their obligations to consult widely are less great, and they are less vulnerable to direct political retribution.

Erosion of the ability of private colleges and universities to compete with their public counterparts is no hypothetical concern or nameless fear either. The effects of the Tax Reform Act of 1986 are likely to be substantial. Even more ominous, however, are the political attitudes that surfaced in connection with consideration of the tax bill—namely, that many private institutions are "rich" or "just another business" and thus do not deserve the consideration due the public institutions "because they are not public." What does "rich" mean compared to the taxing power of the state? Indeed, financial strength is a necessary condition for political independence. And is not the value of an institution more closely related to its mission and performance than its funding mix?

The effort to broaden the tax base is not over, and private higher education remains a tempting target. Clapp (this volume) gives one example: the possibility of even stricter limitations on tax-exempt bonds. Another example can be found in the announcement of new congressional hearings on the unrelated business income tax; it includes the question, "Should endowment income be exempt from tax?" (Committee on Ways and Means, 1986, paragraph II.C). The movement into nontraditional income-generating activities will fan the flames. The predicted lobbying efforts by state governors on behalf of higher education, as welcome as they will be, are not likely to enhance the ability of private institutions to compete with their public counterparts.

Private higher education is too important to be sacrificed to government's short-run financial exigencies or to political logrolling. Nor should federal policy with respect to competition in higher education be determined by the uncoordinated interaction of other priorities. The development of such policy is an important matter that deserves attention on its merits.

References

Committee on Ways and Means, U.S. House of Representatives. *Press Release no. 25*. Washington, D.C.: Government Printing Office, 1986.

Hopkins, D.S.P., and Massy, W. F. *Planning Models for Colleges and Universities.* Stanford, Calif.: Stanford University Press, 1981.

National Science Board, Office of Science and Technology Policy, Government-University-Industry Research Roundtable. *Academic Research Facilities: Financing Strategies.* Washington, D.C.: National Academy Press, 1986.

Rosenzweig, R. M. "Public and Private Universities: Much Alike, Usefully Different." In L. W. Koepplin and D. A. Wilson (eds.), *The Future of State Universities.* New Brunswick, N.J.: Rutgers University Press, 1985.

Simon, J. G. "Research on Philanthropy." Paper delivered at the twenty-fifth anniversary conference of the National Conference on Philanthropy, Denver, Col., November 8, 1979.

William F. Massy is vice-president for business and finance at Stanford University.

Index

A

Academic facilities, financial planning for, 92
Academic freedom, and research partnerships, 74-75
Alternative minimum tax (AMT): and bond market, 38; and charitable contributions, 78, 92, 98; and family income, 10; and property contributions, 13, 14
American Municipal Bond Assurance Corporation (AMBAC), 40
Anderson, R. E., 2, 8, 9, 20
Arbitrage, requirements for, 36-37
Arbitrage income: concept of, 16, 36; and tax-exempt leasing, 50
Arkansas, capital needs in, 26
Association of American Universities, 22, 31
Average deferral percentage (ADP), and nondiscrimination rules, 18

B

Bargain sale to charity, 80-81
Bernard, C., 2, 9, 20
Boeckh Construction Index, 24
Bond Investors Guaranty Corporation, 40
Bond market: analysis of, 33-40; and arbitrage requirements and reserve restrictions, 36-37; conclusions on, 38-40; corporate and municipal, 93; and financing considerations, 37-38; and governmental use and private activity bonds, 33-35; and private activity limit and costs of issuance, 35-36; and refundings, 37; and tax-exempt items, 38

C

California, synergy in, 23
California, University of, capital needs of, 25
Capital: cost of, 94-95; financial planning for, 94-97; forms of, 2; for higher education purposes, 88-90; sources of, 89-90; uses of, 88-89
Capital needs: analysis of, 21-31; background on, 3-4, 21-23; conclusions on, 29-31; determining, 24-27; institutional plan of action for, 30; for physical plant expenditures and assets, 23-24; purposes for determining, 21-22; for research facilities and equipment, 27-29
Catch-up contributions, and tax reform, 18
Centers of Advanced Technology, 23
Charitable contributions: and alternative minimum tax, 78, 92, 98; and tax reform, 13-14
Clapp, D. C., 4, 14, 33, 40, 93, 101
Clifford Trusts, 91
College Construction Loan Insurance Association, 39
Columbia University: capital needs of, 26; science and technology loans to, 23
Commission for Higher Education (Indiana), 26
Committee on Ways and Means, 83-84, 101
Compliance costs, and tax reform, 12, 19
Confidentiality, and research partnerships, 74-75
Consumer Price Index, 24, 54
Cornell University, science and technology loans to, 23
Corrallo, S., 8
Cost of carry, and bond market, 38
Credit ratings, and bond market, 38

D

Davies, J., 5, 77, 86, 88, 89
Debt: background on, 4; as capital source, 90; or equity financing, 95-97; financial planning for structure of, 92-94; and tax reform, 14-16

Deferred compensation and retirement benefits, and tax reform, 17-18
Derek, J. C., 8
Detroit, University of, and tuition prepayment plan, 57
Duquesne University, and tuition prepayment plan, 57, 59

E

Eden, C.G.H., 4, 41, 51, 90, 95
Endowment income, and tax reform, 16-17
Equipment contributions, and tax reform, 14
Equity financing: or debt, 95-97; with real estate, 77-86; with research partnerships, 67-76
Essentiality, and tax-exempt leasing, 45
Estates and gifts, and tax reform, 14
Executive Office of the President, 31
Expenditures: for physical plant, 23-24; and tax reform, 17-19

F

Faculty: housing for, and tax reform, 18-19, 89, 99; rewards for, and research, 70, 74
Family income, and tax reform, 9-10
Financial aid, and tax reform, 11-12, 98
Financial Guaranty Insurance Corporation, 40
Financial planning: for academic facilities, 92; analysis of, 87-102; background on, 7-8, 87; for capital, 94-97; for debt structure, 92-94; integrated, 90-94; and nontraditional income opportunities, 88; for operations, 91-92; and tax reform, 97-101
Financing: and bond market, 33-40; and capital needs, 21-31; with equity, 67-86; new view of, 1-2; planning of, 87-102; and tax-exempt leasing, 41-51; and tax reform, 9-20; with tuition prepayment plans, 53-65
Forum for College Financing Alternatives, 2

Franck, G., 2, 8, 9, 20
Fuqua, D., 22

G

Goldstein, M. B., 5, 67, 76, 88, 90, 100
Government-University-Industry Research Roundtable, 102
Governmental appropriations, and tax reform, 16. *See also* State governments

H

Hansen, J. S., 55, 65
Hart, L., 5, 53, 65, 91
Hartle, T. W., 54, 65
Higher education: analysis of tax reform and, 9-20; and bond market, 33-40; capital needs in, 21-31, 88-90; diversification needed in, 78-79; and equity financing, 67-86; expenditures for, 17-19; financial planning for, 87-102; investment strategies in, 77-78; and knowledge, sale of, 67-68; licensing and royalties for, 68-69; real estate equity financing in, 77-86; in research partnerships, 67-76; revenues for, 9-17; and sponsored research, 69-70; subsidiaries and intermediaries in, 73-74; tax-exempt leasing for, 41-51; and tax exemptions, 84-86; and tuition prepayment plans, 53-65
Hopkins, D.S.P., 87, 91, 102
H. R. 2823, 22
Housing, faculty, and tax reform, 18-19, 89, 99

I

Indiana, capital needs in, 26
Individual Retirement Account (IRA), 18, educational, 59
Interest deductibility for education loans, 98-99
Internal Revenue Code, 9, 19, 85; Section 103 of, 41, 42, 43, 46, 50; Section 401(a) of, 99; Section 401(k) of, 17-18; Section 403(b) of, 3, 17-18; Section 415 of, 18; Section 501(c)(3)

of, 15, 34-35, 36, 37, 38, 39, 98, 99; Section 2503(c) of, 10-11; Section 3121(b)(10) of, 12
Internal Revenue Service (IRS), 12, 15, 59, 62, 64, 85
Iowa, capital needs in, 26

J

Joint Committee on Taxation, 38
Joint Economic Committee, 55
Joint venture partnerships, and real estate equity financing, 82-83

K

Kaiser, H. H., 3, 21, 31, 88
Kansas, capital needs in, 26

L

Leverage, and capital planning, 95-97
L. F. Rothschild Unterberg Towbin, 94
Liability, and research partnerships, 72-73
Licensing, for higher education, 68-69
Loans, and tax reform, 11

M

Marginal tax rates, reduction of, 13
Maryland, University of, capital needs of, 26
Massachusetts: synergy in, 23; tuition prepayment plan in, 57-58
Massy, W. F., 7, 87, 91, 102
Meyerson, J. W., 8
Michigan, tuition prepayment plan in, 57-58, 60, 61
Moody's, 48
Moynihan, D. P., 2
Municipal Bond Insurance Association, 40
Municipal lease/purchase financing. *See* Tax-exempt leasing

N

National Association of College and University Business Officers, 23
National Association of Securities Dealers, 49
National Center for Postsecondary Governance and Financing, 2
National Science Board, 88, 102
National Science Foundation (NSF), 3, 22, 27-28, 29, 31
New Jersey, tuition prepayment plan in, 57-58
New York: capital needs in, 26; technology grants and loans in, 23
Nonappropriation, in tax-exempt leasing, 43-44
Nondiscrimination, and tax reform, 17-18
Nonsubstitution, in tax-exempt leasing, 44
North Carolina: capital needs in, 25; synergy in, 23

O

Office of Education Research and Improvement (OERI), 1n, 8
Office of the Comptroller of the Currency, 46
Office of Science and Technology Policy, 102
Operations, financial planning for, 91-92

P

Participating leases and loans, and real estate equity financing, 81-82
Participation certificates, and tax-exempt leasing, 49-50
Pensions, and tax reform, 17-18, 99
Physical plant, capital needs for, 23-24
Private institutions: affordability of, 54-55; and bond market, 34-35, 39; and capital needs for research facilities, 28-29; and debt financing, 15-16; Robin Hood effect at, 56; and tax reform, 98, 100-101
Property contributions, and tax reform, 13-14, 80-81

R

Rating criteria, for tax-exempt leasing, 45-46
Real estate equity financing: analysis of, 77-86; approaches to, 79-83;

Real Estate Equity Financing *(continued)*
  background on, 5-6, 77-78; and participating arrangements, 81-83; and real estate contributions, 13-14, 80-81; risks and trade-offs of, 83; summary on, 86; tax problems in, 83-86
Refundings, and bond market, 37
Research facilities, capital needs for, 27-29
Research partnership equity financing: analysis of, 67-76; background on, 6-7; benefits and drawbacks of, 71-73; as capital source, 90; and confidentiality, 74-75; described, 70-71; and faculty rewards, 74; and liability, 72-73; mechanisms for, 75-76; subsidiaries and intermediaries for, 73-74
Research and experimentation (R&E) credit, and tax reform, 14, 99-100
Research Triangle Park, 23
Retirement, and tax reform, 17-18, 99
Revenues, and tax reform, 9-17
Rosenzweig, R. M., 100-101, 102
Route 128, 23
Royalties, for higher education, 68-69

S

Savings, and tax reform, 10-12
Savings Bonds, Series EE, 11
Scholarships and fellowships, and tax reform, 11-12, 98
Securities Act of 1933, 46
Securities and Exchange Commission, 46, 49, 93
Securities Exchange Act of 1934, 46
Securities laws, and tax-exempt leasing, 46
Security interest, and tax-exempt leasing, 45
Silicon Valley, 23
Simon, J.G., 100, 102
Standard & Poor's Corporation, 45, 48
Standard tuition units, 58, 61, 63
Stanford University: financial planning at, 87, 91-94, 98; research partnerships of, 90
State Board for Higher Education (Maryland), 26
State governments: and capital needs, 22-23, 25, 28-29, 90; and tax reform, 16; and tuition prepayment plans, 57-58
Step transaction doctrine, and real estate equity financing, 85
Students: dependent and independent, 10, 12; international, 19
Subsidiaries, for research partnerships, 73-74
Syracuse University: capital needs of, 26; science and technology loans to, 23

T

Task Force on Higher Education Finance, 34, 35, 40
Tax-exempt bonds: and research facilities, 28-29; and tax reform, 98
Tax-Exempt Commercial Paper, 37
Tax-exempt conditional sale financing. *See* Tax-exempt leasing
Tax-exempt leasing: analysis of, 41-51; background on, 4-5, 41-42; benefits of, 47-48; as capital source, 90; conclusions on, 50-51; and essentiality, 45; and market trends, 48-49; and master lease, 49; and nonappropriation, 43-44; and nonsubstitution, 44; and participation certificates, 49-50; rating criteria for, 45-46; and real estate equity financing, 85-86; rules for, 43; and securities laws, 46; and security interest, 45; and tax considerations, 42-43; workings of, 46-47
Tax-exempt status: and bond market, 38; and real estate equity financing, 84; and tuition prepayment plans, 59-60, 62-63
Tax reform: analysis of, 9-20; background on, 2-3; and bond market, 33-40; and capital needs, 21-31; and charitable contributions, 13-14, 78, 92, 98; conclusions on, 19-20; and debt financing, 14-16; and endowment income, 16-17; and equity financing, 67-86; and expenditures, 17-19; and faculty housing, 18-19, 89, 99; and financial planning, 87-102; and government appropria-

tions, 16; and retirement, 17-18, 99; and revenues, 9-17; and tax-exempt leasing, 41-51; and tuition and fees, 9-13, 53-65

Tax Reform Act of 1986: and bond market, 33-40; and financial planning, 87, 97-101; and higher education, 9-20, 97-100; impact of, 2, 4, 8, 97; and real estate investments, 78, 80-81; and research partnerships, 72; and tax-exempt leasing, 41-51; and tuition prepayment, 53, 56, 60, 61

Texas College and University System, capital needs of, 25

Thomas, R., 5, 77, 86, 88, 89

Tuition: and remission benefits, 12, 99; and tax reform, 9-13, 53-65

Tuition prepayment plans: and affordability factors, 53-58; analysis of, 53-65; background on, 5; conclusions on, 64; and financial planning, 91-92, 97; financial risks of, 63-64; limitations of, 55-56; marketing of, 63; national program for, 58; and needs of students and colleges, 56; for single college, 57; state programs for, 57-58; tax advantages of, 59-60, 62-63; transferability of, 61; withdrawal issues for, 60-63

U

Uniform Gifts to Minors Act, 10, 56

U.S. Congress: and bond market, 38, 39, 40; and capital needs, 22, 27; and endowment income, 101; and real estate equity financing, 83-84, 86; and tax-exempt leasing, 50; and tuition financing, 55, 59

U.S. Department of Education, 1n, 8

U.S. Department of Treasury, 35, 38, 50, 57, 99

Unrelated business taxable income (UBTI): and private institutions, 101; and research partnerships, 72

Unrelated trade or business income (UTBI): and real estate ventures, 84-85

V

Variable Rate Demand Notes (VRDNs), 37

W

White House Science Council on the Health of U.S. Colleges and Universities, 22, 30, 31

Wofford, D., 8

Ministry of Education, Ontario
Information Centre, 13th Floor,
Mowat Block, Queen's Park,
Toronto, Ont.   M7A 1L2